William Wordsworth

Updated Edition

Twayne's English Authors Series

Herbert Sussman, editor

Northeastern University

TEAS 118

WILLIAM WORDSWORTH
Portrait by B. R. Haydon
Couresty of the National Portrait Gallery, London

William Wordsworth

Updated Edition

Russell Noyes

Updated by
John O. Hayden
University of California, Davis

Twayne Publishers
A Division of G. K. Hall & Co. • *Boston*

Noyes, Russell, 1901–
William Wordsworth

William Wordsworth, Updated Edition
Russell Noyes
Updated by John O. Hayden

Copyright 1991 by G. K. Hall & Co.
All rights reserved.
Published by Twayne Publishers
A division of G. K. Hall & Co.
70 Lincoln Street
Boston, Massachusetts 02111

Copyediting supervised by Barbara Sutton.
Book production by Gabrielle B. McDonald.
Typeset in Garamond by Compositors Corporation of Cedar Rapids, Iowa.

10 9 8 7 6 5 4 3 2 1

Library of Congress Cataloging-in-Publication Data

Noyes, Russell, 1901–
    William Wordsworth / Russell Noyes ; updated by John O. Hayden. —
Updated ed.
        p.   cm. — (Twayne's English authors series ; TEAS 118)
    Includes bibliographical references and index.
    ISBN 0-8057-7002-X (alk. paper)
    1. Wordsworth, William, 1770–1850—Criticism and interpretation.
I. Hayden, John O.   II. Title.   III. Series.
PR5888.N69   1991
821′.7—dc20   90-46239
                                                           CIP

To Vernice

Contents

Preface

Russell Noyes's volume on William Wordsworth is generally acknowledged to be among the best in Twayne's English Authors Series. Thus, to revise it gave me pleasure as well as a sense of responsibility.

By producing a short biography of the poet, Noyes worked at a fairly high level of generalization. Therefore, newly unearthed factual details have had little impact on his account, although some revisions have been necessary. As for new critical viewpoints, where a greater role for personal judgment obtains, I have kept changes to a minimum, and these are most often reflected in the notes.

Wordsworth scholarship as a whole has made vast strides since 1971; a number of new editions—especially the ongoing Cornell editions of the poetry and the Oxford edition of the prose—have changed the face of research. And many new scholarly studies of Wordsworth's views, especially of his visionary interests, have been produced. I have brought many of these new efforts into the bibliography, although it was necessary to limit new items to the best and most useful.

I have also made stylistic revisions in the interest of tone and clarity. Although the substance of Noyes's text for the most part stands as it was, two sections have been totally rewritten. My treatment of *The Borderers* replaces an emphasis on intellectual influences with a more pertinent look at what Wordsworth himself had to say about the psychology of morality of the play. The section on the Preface to *Lyrical Ballads* largely reorders Noyes's comments by centering the discussion on alternative modern views.

My goal in all the revisions, both deletions and additions, has been to produce a still more useful introductory volume to Wordsworth's life and works. It is my hope that William Wordsworth emerges as the very great poet and thinker he was.

JOHN O. HAYDEN

University of California, Davis

Preface to First Edition

The aim of this book is to examine critically those poems of Wordsworth that have endured the sifting of time. The life of the author, the sources and analogues of his poems, the circumstances and progress of their composition, and other information useful to this central purpose are given. Biographical and other pertinent facts are presented in chronological sequence as they unfold in a meaningful pattern to show Wordsworth's development and achievement as a poet.

Thus chapter 1 opens with a picture, given to us by Wordsworth himself, of a babe in arms being nurtured by the "ceaseless music" of the Derwent River. The chapter continues with an account of the gifts received from his mother and father, and of the ministering gentleness of his sister. It tells of the young boy's driving power and stubborn energy and of his awesome experiences in solitary places. It fills in important events in his schoolboy days at Hawkshead and tells of his friendships there. Then the story moves forward to Wordsworth's life at Cambridge, to summer vacations including the momentous tour of the Alps with Jones, to London after college, to France and the revolution and his involvement with Annette Vallon, again to London, where we find him in the throes of doubt and despair, finally to Racedown with Dorothy and the poet's slow recovery. Out of the pattern of these circumstances one sees the poet moving from early experimentation and imitation in *An Evening Walk* and *Descriptive Sketches* to "Guilt and Sorrow" and *The Borderers* until his way is cleared and his art is matured in "The Ruined Cottage."

Subsequent chapters carry forward the account of Wordsworth's poetic advance. Attention is paid to the prose where it opens up his poetic intentions and sheds light upon those accomplishments. Chapter 2 tells of the friendship of Wordsworth and Coleridge and of their history-making collaboration in the creation of *Lyrical Ballads*. Chapter 3 tells of the potent release of creative energy stirred by recollection, while the poet was in Germany, which resulted in the new kind of poetry that went into the second volume of *Lyrical Ballads* (1800). Chapter 4, central in many ways, offers an account of the origin and composition of *The Prelude*, Wordsworth's masterpiece, of its themes and ideas, and of its language, structure, and style. Chapter 5 tells of crucial happenings in Wordsworth's life during the years 1802 to 1807 and of how *Poems in Two Volumes* (1807) reflect them. Chapter 6 offers an account of Wordsworth's once-esteemed, but now neglected, *The Excursion*; this chapter also has something to say about the reasons for the poet's fading powers and about the poems of his later period. The final chapter summarizes Wordsworth's shortcomings and excellences and evaluates his achievement as a great, original genius.

More has been written about Wordsworth than about any other English author except Shakespeare. Many of the books and articles about him are, of course, excellent and of great usefulness to the beginning student as well as to the expert. The most worthwhile among them are given in the Selected Bibliography together with evaluations that should be helpful. Wordsworth has been reappraised by each generation of readers beginning with his own, and controversy is still whirling about him on a number of issues. His genius is of such magnitude that it raises more questions than one can expect to be settled. In his own day, the "simple" Wordsworth was ridiculed for his simpleness, but he is now acclaimed by some for that very quality. In his lifetime he was censured by Keats for the limitation of what Keats called the "egotistical sublime"; but Wordsworth's defenders insist that his reach to the sublime, though intimately personal, did not limit him from translating the power of vision to an encompassing love of his fellow men.

To Shelley and Browning, Wordsworth was the "lost leader," a renegade to his earlier republican faith, but Mary Moorman, James K. Chandler, and others have undertaken to put that once fashionable platitude about the poet out of style. Over the years a wide divergence of opinion has also prevailed about the character and value of Wordsworth's mystic faith and his teaching about nature. Scholars like J. W. Beach and Basil Willey were among the skeptics, but Alfred N. Whitehead made a spirited defense of Wordsworth's natural philosophy as viewed in our scientific age. Today, new insights are being offered about the psychology of Wordsworth's creative imagination. And so the search for meaning and understanding goes forward.

My pursuit of meaning in Wordsworth's poetry has continued in and out of the classroom for more than three decades. The results of this long search are presented in these pages. Acknowledgment of my debt to published scholarship may be understood to include those works listed in the Selected Bibliography, but some books and articles that have been of unusual importance or influence in points of interpretation are singled out for special mention in the Notes and References. I wish especially to acknowledge the stimulus and challenge of students in my classes over the years, both undergraduate and graduate, who have called for, and in a considerable measure helped to bring, clarity and insight into meaning wherever it is found in this study.

For kind permission to reprint portions of critical commentary made by myself on some half-dozen of Wordsworth's poems first appearing in *Wordsworth and the Art of Landscape* (1968) I wish to thank the Indiana University Press. For most excellent editorial criticism and advice I am grateful to Professor Sylvia Bowman.

My greatest obligation is to my wife, Vernice Lockridge Noyes, who has been a sympathetic and discerning critic of my labors, and who has typed this manuscript.

RUSSELL NOYES

Indiana University

Chronology

1770   William Wordsworth, second son of John Wordsworth, a lawyer, and Anne (Cookson), born 7 April at Cockermouth in Cumberland.

1778–1787   Mother dies and the family is dispersed; Wordsworth is sent to lodge with Ann Tyson both at Colthouse and in Hawkshead, where he attends the village grammar school. His schoolmaster, William Taylor, encourages him to write verses.

1783   Father dies, leaving his five children in the guardianship of their uncles.

1787–1791   Attends St. John's College, Cambridge. Spends two summer holidays in the Lake Country and a third (1790) on a walking tour with Robert Jones through France and Switzerland and across the Alps into Italy.

1791   Receives bachelor of arts degree from Cambridge; goes to London; then to France (November).

1792   In Orleans (winter and fall), has an affair with Annette Vallon, who bears him a daughter, Caroline; in Blois (spring and summer), meets Michel Beaupuy and becomes a convert to French republicanism. Returns to England (December).

1793   *An Evening Walk* and *Descriptive Sketches* published; takes walking tour over Salisbury Plain and into Wales (visits Tintern Abbey in the Wye valley).

1794   Moves about living with relatives and friends.

1795   Bequest of £900 from Raisley Calvert enables Wordsworth to establish a home with his sister Dorothy at Racedown farmhouse in Dorsetshire. Plunges into extensive reading of modern European literature.

1796–1797   Composes *The Borderers,* a five-act drama, and "The Ruined Cottage."

1797–1798   Settles with Dorothy at Alfoxden, Somersetshire, to be near Coleridge in Nether Stowey. Close collaboration with

Coleridge results in *Lyrical Ballads*. Revisits the Wye valley and Tintern Abbey with Dorothy.

1799   Lives in Goslar, Germany, during a bitterly cold but poetically productive winter. Writes the Lucy poems and books 1 and 2 of *The Prelude*. Settles with Dorothy at Dove Cottage, Grasmere, their principal residence until 1808.

1800   Writes the great fragment of *The Recluse,* "Michael," and many other poems. Coleridge's residence at nearby Keswick allows for frequent intercourse between Wordsworth and Coleridge.

1801   Wordsworth's creative power is in temporary subsidence.

1802   Year opens with a resurgence of productive energy, which continues with few and short interruptions until 1807. Composes part of the great "Ode: Intimations of Immortality," many of his best sonnets, and numerous fine lyrics. In late summer, travels with Dorothy to Calais; spends a month visiting with Annette and Caroline. Marries Mary Hutchinson (4 October).

1803   Tour of Scotland with Dorothy results in a series of poems. Spends a week with Walter Scott. Friendship and patronage of Sir George Beaumont begins in this year and continues until Sir George's death in 1827.

1804   Continues composing *The Prelude*, which is completed in 1805.

1805   His brother John drowns in the wreck of his vessel, the *Abergavenny*.

1807   *Poems in Two Volumes* is published and attacked in the *Edinburgh Review* and other periodicals.

1808   Moves to Allan Bank, Grasmere.

1809   Publishes *The Convention of Cintra,* a political tract.

1810   Becomes estranged from Coleridge (reconciled in 1812). *A Description of the Scenery of the Lakes* is published.

1813   Appointed Distributor of Stamps for Westmoreland. Moves to Rydal Mount.

1814   *The Excursion* published.

1815   *Collected Poems* and *The White Doe of Rylstone* (written in 1807) published.

1819   *Peter Bell* (written in 1798) and *The Waggoner* (written in 1805) published.

1820   *The River Duddon*, a series of sonnets, published.

1822   *Memorials of a Tour of the Continent* and *Ecclesiastical Sketches* published.

1835   *Yarrow Revisited, and Other Poems* published.

1839   Receives honorary doctorate from Oxford.

1842   *Poems Chiefly of Early and Late Years* published. Resigns as Stamp Distributor and receives a pension of £300 per annum from the Civil List.

1843   Succeeds Robert Southey as poet laureate.

1849–1850   The seventh and last collected edition of the *Poems*, edited by Wordsworth, is published in six volumes.

1850   Dies at Rydal Mount 23 April and is buried in Grasmere churchyard. *The Prelude*, revised mainly in 1839, is published posthumously.

Chapter One

The Making of the Poet

Childhood at Cockermouth

Wordsworth's poetic life began, he tells us in *The Prelude,* on the banks of the Derwent in Cockermouth, when, even as a babe in arms, the river was an influence stretching back beyond the gates of conscious memory, a presence that

> lov'd
> To blend his murmurs with my Nurse's song,
> And from his alder shades and rocky falls,
> And from his fords and shallows, sent a voice
> That flow'd along my dreams.

The sound of running water, he often felt, was almost part of his own being, and in aftertime he thanked the Derwent for this first gift of "ceaseless music." At five years of age he was bathing in that stream and making sport long summer days along its banks, like "a naked savage."

Within his spacious home on High Street his mother gave him the priceless gift of tenderness and love. Wordsworth in after years, in *The Prelude,* attributes to the mother the archetype from which springs the happiness of the child's intercourse with the universe: "From this beloved Presence, there exists/A virtue which irradiates and exalts/All objects through all intercourse of sense." His own mother first introduced him to nature; and, when her presence was withdrawn, the boy transferred to nature the affection and devotion he had felt for her. To his father, he owned one great debt: Mr. Wordsworth cared for English poetry and encouraged his son William to learn by heart "large portions of Shakespeare, Milton, and Spenser."

The boy Wordsworth had a driving power and a stubborn energy. He was, he tells us, "of a stiff, moody, and violent temper." He once struck his whip through a family portrait, after first daring his brother Richard to do so. And once, in a frenzy, he went up to the attic of his grandfather's house with the intention of killing himself with one of the foils kept there. His mother said he was the only one of her children about whose future she was anxious; he would be remarkable for good or ill, she said.

In *The Prelude* Wordsworth tells of numerous strange and awesome experiences when fear, shooting across the "coarser pleasures" of his boyhood and their "glad animal movements," became a potent ministrant in shaping his poetic mind. The earliest of these "spots of time," which may serve as representative of others, occurred when he was only five years old. When he was riding with his father's servant near Penrith Beacon, he somehow became separated from his guide. Uncertain where he was, he dismounted and led his pony to a hollow, where he found an old moldering gibbet post and at its foot some initials carved in the turf. He recognized the spot as that upon which a murder had been committed, and, as was the custom of the times, where the murderer had been hanged. At once he fled up the hill, half-faint with terror, till he could see the beacon summit and a girl carrying a pitcher on her head and forcing her way with difficulty against the wind.

> It was, in truth,
> An ordinary sight; but I should need
> Colours and words that are unknown to man
> To paint the visionary dreariness [of that scene.]

Through this adventure in that wild and haunted place, and others like it to follow, the child, not yet six, felt the imaginative awe in the presence of mystery which solitude and solitary things habitually evoked in the man.

Counterbalancing his wildness and turbulence, and supporting the tenderness of his mother, was the gentleness of his sister Dorothy. In the poems celebrating the early years of his life, Wordsworth keeps returning to the softness of her nature. When together they discovered by chance a sparrow's nest, "She looked at it and seemed to fear it;/Dreading, tho' wishing, to be near it." When, in their childish play, together they chased the butterfly, he rushed like a very hunter upon the prey, "But she, God love her! feared to brush/The dust from off its wings." Dorothy brought to her brother in later years the gentleness he acknowledged was hers when they were children; she brought, too, other gifts:

> She gave me eyes, she gave me ears;
> And humble cares, and delicate fears;
> A heart, the fountain of sweet tears;
> And love, and thought, and joy.
>   "The Sparrow's Nest"

Schoolboy at Hawkshead

Wordsworth's eight years at Hawkshead, from his tenth to his eighteenth year, contributed riches to the formation of his poetic mind. He attended the grammar school for seven or eight hours a day, but the rest of his existence seems to have been entirely free. Joyously he gave himself up to the amenities surrounding him. He joined his schoolmates in gregarious sports indoors and out, but the adventures that made the deepest impression upon him were those he experienced by himself. When alone, he snared woodcocks, plundered the raven's nest, or reaped the harvest of hazel nuts. Alone, he wandered through the hollows and over the cliffs, embarked by boat upon the lakes, and followed the rivers to their sources on the lonesome mountain peaks. Swiftly the whole of the countryside became his inheritance. All scenes "beauteous and majestic" became "habitually dear, and all/Their hues and forms were by invisible links/Allied to the affections."

In his fourteenth year Wordsworth first became conscious of loving "words in tuneful order"; he "found them sweet/For their own sake, a passion and a power." His schoolmaster, William Taylor, encouraged him in the writing of poetry; and he composed, at Taylor's request, lines celebrating the bicentenary of the school's founding. This exercise put it into his head "to compose verses from the impulse of [his] own mind." Taylor seems to have had a taste for such eighteenth-century poets as Thomas Gray, William Collins, Thomas Chatterton, and James Beattie—poets who quickly became the favorites of the young Wordsworth.

Of what survives of Wordsworth's youthful verse one poem stands out: "The Vale of Esthwaite," which he describes as a "long poem running on my own adventures and the scenery of the country in which I was brought up." Essentially a topographical poem, written in the eight-syllable meter of Milton's "L'Allegro" and "Il Penseroso," it describes Esthwaite valley and surrounding places, with an intermingling of Gothic passages after the fashion of the day. What distinguishes the poem as unusually promising is the vivid recording of many directly observed images of the landscape. Wordsworth in his seventy-third year told Miss Fenwick, when he was dictating notes about *An Evening Walk,* that he recollected the time and place where most of them were noticed. Wordsworth mentioned as an example the instance of the shepherd dog barking and bounding among the rocks to intercept the sheep, an action of which he was eyewitness for the first time while crossing the Pass of Dunmail Raise. Also he recalled distinctly, he said, the very spot where the image of the darkening boughs and leaves of the oak tree, "fronting the bright west," first struck him: "It was in the way between Hawkshead and Ambleside and gave me extreme pleasure." He also remarked that "The moment was important in my poetical history; for I date from it my consciousness of the infinite variety of natural appearances which had been unnoticed by the poets of any age or country, so far as I was acquainted with them, and I made a resolution to supply, in some degree, the deficiency."[1]

Cambridge and *An Evening Walk*

In the autumn of 1787 Wordsworth exchanged the hardy simplicity of Hawkshead for the comparative luxury of life at St. John's College, Cambridge. At the time of his entrance, Cambridge was a place of idleness and intellectual languor, although St. John's was reputed the best of the colleges. Wordsworth was thrilled at his arrival, but from the first the lectures and examinations failed to interest him. He loved companionship and moved easily "into the weekday works of youth" that surrounded him, drifting aimlessly and reading "lazily in lazy books." But he possessed also an inner integrity, one greater than that of the world he was living in, that left a strangeness in his mind, a feeling that he "was not for that hour,/ Nor for that place."

For his first summer vacation Wordsworth returned to Hawkshead and soon discovered that his year's absence had wrought great changes in himself. He now began consciously to look at both man and nature with a "humanheartedness" so new that it felt like the dawn of another sense. He looked with "clearer knowledge" upon the simple dalefolk he had known as a schoolboy—the quiet woodman, the shepherd on the hills, and even his old dame nodding over her Bible. A lonely encounter with a vagrant soldier met at night upon the highway, who was in need of his help and whom he left in comfort, made a solemn impression upon him that banished all thoughts of frivolity from his mind and gave a new direction to his approach to "the problem of humanity."

The climaxing event of this summer, and one of the most momentous of his life, came to Wordsworth as he returned home at dawn from a night of "dancing, gaiety, and mirth." On his two-mile walk home he had reached some high ground just as the sun was rising, and the wondrous beauty of the morning broke upon him. The shock of sudden removal from excited companionship with "spirits upon the stretch" into brooding solitude caused his mind to leap forward into full communion with the beauty before him:

> Magnificent
> The morning was, in memorable pomp,
> More glorious than I ever had beheld.
> The Sea was laughing at a distance; all
> The solid Mountains were as bright as clouds,
> Grain-tinctured, drench'd in empyrean light;
> And, in the meadows and the lower grounds,
> Was all the sweetness of a common dawn,
> Dews, vapours, and the melody of birds,
> And Labourers going forth into the fields.
> —Ah! need I say, dear Friend, that to the brim
> My heart was full; I made no vows, but vows
> Were then made for me; bond unknown to me
> Was given, that I should be, else sinning greatly,
> A dedicated Spirit.
>
> (*The Prelude,* book 4)

His "moment at sunrise" was not a conscious dedication by Wordsworth to the vocation of poet. The bond given to him was "unknown." Nevertheless, events proved it to be a prophetic blessedness that sustained him for many years.

On his return to college Wordsworth was less attracted to "indolent and vague society," and he withdrew into his own life of feeling and of thought. Authorship now seemed less presumptuous; and, during his second and third winters at Cambridge, it became his practice, he says, to retire after dark into the college garden, where he paced up and down its "Groves and Tributary walks" in the throes of poetic composition. During his second summer vacation he visited Dorothy at Forncett, where she was living with her uncle William Cookson, and made various trips on foot through the north of England. For the last month of his holiday (from mid-September to mid-October) he stayed at Hawkshead, where he continued and probably completed *An Evening Walk,* a poem of nearly four hundred and fifty lines.

An Evening Walk, a topographical poem in heroic couplets, was offered to the reading public as an album of beautiful landscape scenes, chiefly of several Wordsworthian rambles around Lake Windermere. The scenery is described in accordance with the principles of the "picturesque" school of topographical poets, such as Erasmus Darwin and William Rogers, and of the famous delineator of "picturesque" scenes William Gilpin. *An Evening Walk* borrows many images from "The Vale of Esthwaite" and continues Wordsworth's resolution, begun in that poem, to supply in poetical form an abundant variety of directly observed natural appearances. Wordsworth's scenes are rooted in reality; the village murmurs arise from his own Hawkshead.[2] However, Wordsworth reminds his readers that "the plan of his poem has not been confined to a particular walk or place"; for he was "unwilling to submit the poetic spirit to the chains of fact and real circumstances."

The poem is structured around the picturesque variations of landscape revealed by the gradations of evening light—sunset, twilight, and moonlight. Human and animal inhabitants are not excluded; the shepherds and their dogs, the muleteers and their trains, the peasant and his horse, and the majestic swans—all enhance the pastoral scene. The swans, in particular, reflect the idyllic character of their natural surroundings. The swan's bower, "where leafy shades fence off the blustering gale," is described in terms paralleling a peaceful shepherd's cottage. Contrasting with the idyllic life of the swan and her brood is the beggar woman and her starving children who are at the mercy of cruel storms and freezing weather. She serves as a suffering figure reflecting Wordsworth's newly awakened humanitarian interest in the sufferings of the poor.

But the social accent in *An Evening Walk* hardly ruffles the placid surface of its sequence of picturesque descriptions. Having expressed his sympathy for innocence in distress, Wordsworth returns to his description of the charms of evening and concludes his poem with its finest passage in which he joins man and nature in a magnificent manipulation of the images of sound. *An Evening Walk* is the work of a young poet: the imagery is overloaded and often obscured by affectations of manner and style. But, for all its faults, the poem has a freshness, a vitality, and an accuracy in its images that are derived from personal observation. These qualities mark the poem as an early work of genius.

Tour of the Alps, France, and *Descriptive Sketches*

During the long vacation between Wordsworth's junior and senior years at St. John's College, when he should have been studying for his comprehensive examinations, he left for a walking tour of France and Switzerland with his classmate Robert Jones. His main reason for going was to indulge his passion for natural scenery, especially among the magnificent Swiss Alps: "Nature then was sovereign in my heart,/And mighty forms seizing a youthful Fancy/Had given a charter to irregular hopes." He entered France on the anniversary of the storming of the Bastille and found himself plunged into the flood of revolutionary zeal to which he abandoned himself: "Bliss was it in that dawn to be alive,/But to be young was very Heaven!"

Still Wordsworth was not touched, he says, with "intimate concern" for the revolution. He seems to have been carried away by the abstract ideal of liberty, which would soon have evaporated had not the essentially practical Wordsworth seen that the ideal was grounded in reality. When the tour of the Alps was completed, he returned to Cambridge and in February took his degree without distinction. After some months in London, he returned to France with the professed intention of perfecting his French as qualification for a tutorship. At this time, the transformation of the enthusiast for nature into the full-fledged enthusiast for revolution was soon accomplished.

Wordsworth came to know Captain Michel Beaupuy, one of a band of military officers with republican sympathies stationed at Blois. Beaupuy fed Wordsworth's mind with revolutionary philosophy and showed him the sufferings of the poor under the old regime. When they chanced one day to meet "a hunger-bitten girl" watching over a heifer and when Beaupuy, in agitation, cried out, "'Tis against *that*/That we are fighting," Wordsworth saw the need for the revolution. "Then I became a patriot," he said, "and my heart was all/Given to the people, and my love was theirs." He nearly joined the Girondists (a party of moderates) when he was in Paris, but he was recalled to England by lack of funds and perhaps by pressing personal claims. For Wordsworth had been swept away by other tides. When he was in Orleans he had fallen passionately in love with a dark-eyed French girl, Annette Vallon, who responded to his love and bore him a daughter. His sudden return to England seems to have been partly forced upon him by the necessity of securing funds for their support. He seems to have desired to rejoin Annette; but, when war between England and France broke out, return was impossible.

During his residence in France Wordsworth was at work on *Descriptive Sketches,* a poem in heroic couplets based on his Alpine tour with Jones two years earlier. A loco-descriptive poem of some eight hundred lines, it recounts, in a crowded sequence of sketches, the esthetic pleasures of the pedestrian traveler in the Swiss and Italian Alps. When Wordsworth was on his tour, he wrote Dorothy, he was "a perfect enthusiast" in his admiration for nature in all its forms. In the poem, however, the original feeling of unrestrained enthusiasm is curiously colored by a newly acquired mood from his second visit to France. Wordsworth casts the poet in the role of a melancholy wanderer seeking refuge from love's misery, in all probability a transference of symptoms agitating the lover of Annette. Sections of the poem that describe the scenery of the Italian lakes follow the vogue of the then-popular travel poetry. In the scenes describing Lake Como, for example, there is a well-conducted, harmonious time sequence (that reminds one of *An Evening Walk*) in the passage from sunset to twilight to starlight and to the next morning in the progress of the rising sun. However, there are two types of landscape featured in *Descriptive Sketches:* one is a mild beauty represented by the "delicious scenes" of the Italian lakes; the other, the more awesome beauty of the Alps.

In the high Alps Wordsworth was confronted by nature on a scale mightier and more awe-inspiring than he had hitherto ever dreamed of—and evocative of sensations that approached sublimity. Many scenes vexed his sight and many overwhelmed him; his imagination sought helplessly for an inner vision to rest upon. When he tried to put into words his impressions of the Alps in *Descriptive Sketches,* he leaned heavily upon the writings of two earlier travelers to Switzerland, William Coxe and Ramond de Carbonnières. He used Ramond for scenic details and for vocabulary; but, overall, the Frenchman was not much more than a crutch for Wordsworth to lean on. Boldly, Wordsworth widened the contrasts and multiplied the *locus* of life. Through personification he made a separate (visual) entity of nearly everything his glance encountered. Few single "prospects" satisfied him; he spread the swift interchanges of seasons, times, and landscapes over nature as a whole. Not until ten years later in *The Prelude,* book 6, did he express at last the harmonizing vision of the idea of nature that was haunting his mind. But, as Geoffrey Hartman observes, the distance between *The Prelude,* written in Wordsworth's maturity, and *Descriptive Sketches* is enormous.[3]

On the tour with Jones, Wordsworth had taken pleasure in meditating upon scenes of domestic felicity among the cottagers and upon the freedom of the shepherds in their mountain haunts. But in *Descriptive Sketches* these sentimental reflections are vigorously transposed into Wordsworth's belief in the manifold blessings of the republicanism he had adopted after his summer with Beaupuy. In the poem, he abandons his disguise as a leisurely and observant pedestrian traveler; and he heightens his scenic descriptions with vignettes of "social suffering," tributes to noble statesmen-warriors, and a salute to traces yet remaining in republican Switzerland of a bygone Golden Age. He ends the poem with a vehement prayer that France might ride "Sublime o'er Conquest, Avarice, and Pride"—that she might defeat all enemies of the Republic.

When *Descriptive Sketches* was published in London, a few months after the execution of the French king, its fiery defense of revolutionary freedom stirred the anger of reviewers. However, most readers in the London of 1793 appear to have been indifferent to its subject or discouraged by its inflated obscurities. Coleridge alone recognized occasional flashes of splendor.

Ardent Republican: "Letter to the Bishop of Llandaff" and "Guilt and Sorrow"

Wordsworth returned to England in December (or late November) 1792, "a patriot of the world."[4] For him, the French Revolution was not simply the struggle of a poor people to be free but the dawn of a new day for all mankind. He explains in *The Prelude* that, to him, coming from his free world of shepherds, farmers, and Cambridge students, the revolution seemed nothing out of the natural order. It was the rightful gift to all men of what was already their precious heritage—freedom and equality between man and man. His deep, ingrained love of England, its very soil and its people, had extended itself to a love of France and the French; and personal love had sealed the bond. Then, suddenly in February 1793, England declared war on France, and he was thrown into agonizing mental conflict. He "felt the ravage of this most unnatural strife" in his own heart.

Wordsworth did not yield to despair at once; he wrote a forthright defense of the revolution in reply to a recanting biship, Watson of Llandaff, who formerly had supported the event. Wordsworth's document, entitled "A Letter to the Bishop of Llandaff on the Extraordinary Avowal of his Political Principles . . . by a Republican," was never finished and remained unpublished, probably because his publisher, Joseph Johnson, though a friend of radicals, feared prosecution by the government. For Wordsworth's letter is a direct attack on monarchy, and on the constitution of "Kings and Lords and Commons . . . who have constitutionally the right of enacting whatever laws they please, in defiance of the petitions or remonstrances of the nation." Wordsworth repudiates the bishop's smug satisfaction with things as they are and speaks out, often with an edge of sarcasm, on the extremes of poverty and riches, the prevalent injustices of English law courts, the curse of a hereditary nobility that breeds insolence and wickedness, and a disastrous war instigated by royalty that heaps misery upon the poor. But the interest in the pamphlet lies not so much in the ideas expressed, which were not startlingly original, as in its burning sincerity. Wordsworth, genuinely aroused, pressed his attack, as Émile Legouis rightly says, with "almost religious fervor."

Wordsworth's stay in London was terminated when a wealthy school-fellow, William Calvert, invited him to be his companion on a tour of southern England. They spent a month on the Isle of Wight and were on their way north when Calvert's horse, which was not used to carriage duty, dragged the occupants and their vehicle into a ditch and broke it to shivers. Wordsworth and Calvert both escaped unhurt, but they decided to end the tour. Calvert mounted the horse and rode off to the north of England, leaving Wordsworth alone in the middle of the vast, uninhabitated Salisbury Plain, over which he wandered for two or three days. One of the places his wanderings took him to was Stonehenge, near which, in a mood of exaltation, he had a visionary experience that may be ranked in importance with his "dedication" five years before, during his first vacation. He felt an inrush of faith, never so fully felt before, that he was one of that great company of poets possessed of a "privilege" whereby a work of his, "creative and enduring, may become/A power like one of Nature's."

In his reverie he saw a phantom pageant of the legendary past, "Saw multitudes of men, and here and there,/A single Briton in his wolf-skin vest/With shield and stone-axe, stride across the Wold." He called on darkness, and the pitch black was broken by flames and the sight of human sacrifices being offered up in the flames of the altar. In some odd way, Wordsworth seems to have associated the ancient Britons of his "reverie" with the poor of his own time. As he made his way to the Vale of Clwyd in Wales by way of Bristol and the valley of the Wye, he found himself taking a new interest in the tramps and beggars who were walking the roads with him. Republicanism, which he had learned from Beaupuy, now assumed a new meaning. He began to question and to watch those he met and to hold familiar talk with them. On the long solitary walk from Salisbury Plain to Wales, equality ceased to be a doctrine and became a way of life. From that time, Wordsworth determined he would be the poet of humble life.

The first fruit of this determination was a narrative poem, "Salisbury Plain," composed mentally during his wanderings, written down during the next few weeks, and revised two years later at Racedown. Eventually, again drastically altered, the poem was published in 1842 as "Guilt and Sorrow." In its least complicated form, it is the story of "The Female Vagrant," which was printed in *Lyrical Ballads* in 1798. This version records the tragic life story of a Cumberland woman, now reduced to destitution, which is told during a night storm to a traveler who has lost his way on Salisbury Plain. The traveler clearly owes his descriptions to the wanderings of Wordsworth, who transfers to the poem many images of the bleak Salisbury landscape and reflections of his own depressed and disillusioned mood.

The story itself, he tells us, is a true one told to him a year or two before by the sufferer herself. Her persecution began when a landowner, empowered by the enclosure laws, drove her father from his hereditary farm. An interval of happiness was theirs when she married and her father came to live in her new home. But their respite from sorrow was brief: her father soon died; her husband, forced into idleness by economic pressures, joined the navy. She followed him with their three children across the Atlantic, only to suffer constant distress and finally bleak misery when, in one remorseless year, all but she perished.

In his revision of the poem, which was undertaken in October 1795 and identified in manuscript as "Adventures on Salisbury Plain," Wordsworth extended the picture of injustice and painted the oppressive social conditions in still darker colors. In this version, the vagrant woman's father is prey "to cruel injuries" and persecuted with "wilfull wrong" until he is forced from his land. To the tale of the female vagrant's sufferings Wordsworth added her cruel treatment at the hospital and her homeless wandering after her release. He also added the pitiable story of an impressed sailor who was returning home after service in the American wars. Following his discharge, he was incited by a cruel fraud to commit murder. He confesses the crime to his wife, who, in the last stages of consumption, forgives him and dies in his arms. The sailor then surrenders himself to justice and is publicly "hung on high in iron case."

Into the stories of these three desolate outcasts Wordsworth poured a bitter, unsparing indictment of the dominant class that oppresses the poor and makes them what they are. He exposed corrupt power and privilege, the calamities of war, the cruel impressment of soldiers and sailors, unfeeling charity, the forced perversion of simple hearts, and the horrors of public execution. Underlying Wordsworth's virulent attack on English society were his republican sentiments, already given forceful expression in the closing lines of *Descriptive Sketches* and in the "Letter to the Bishop of Llandaff." But in "Salisbury Plain" he faced more squarely the problem of interpreting social abuses in terms of what he saw and felt. For the first time, he created real characters drawn from the world he knew and identified himself with their experiences and their feelings.

Wordsworth also inserted himself into "Salisbury Plain" in another significant way. The visionary experience he had by the pillars of Stonehenge that obliged him to draw comparisons between the barbarous age of the Druids and "the terrors of our day" spread to encompass his response to the solemn desolation of Salisbury Plain. In his representation of it, Wordsworth provided his poem with the atmosphere of mysterious awe characteristic of the Gothic school of terror. This aestheticism does not, as some critics claim, divide the aesthetic impulse between terror and pity; instead, it enhances what Wordsworth calls in his preface to the poem his "melancholy forebodings" over the distress and misery to which the poor are subject. As he pursued his lonely way along the bare white road almost empty of the signs of man, his loneliness quickened his imagination. With an arresting vividness he paints his desolate scenes, such as the lonely guide post on the waste momentarily revealed by lightning, or the bleakness of the landscape described by stark negations:

> No gipsy cower'd o'er fire of furze or broom;
> No labourer watch'd his red kiln glaring bright,
> Nor taper glimmer'd dim from sick man's room;
> Along the waste no line of mournful light
> From lamp of lonely toll-gate stream'd athwart the night.

What aroused Coleridge's admiration for "Salisbury Plain" when he first read it in 1796 was "the union of deep feeling with profound thought; the fine balance of truth in observing, with the imaginative faculty in modifying, the objects observed, and above all the original gift of spreading the tone, the atmosphere, and with it the depth and height of the ideal world around forms, incidents and situations, of which, for the common view, custom had bedimmed all the lustre."[5] Coleridge's claims are excessive, but they do indicate, with discrimination and accuracy, what Wordsworth's intentions in poetry were at the time and those features that would distinguish his poetry in the future.

William Godwin and Godwinism: *The Borderers*

Not long after Wordsworth's return from France, a change occurred in his thinking about the revolution. A year of bloody excesses under Robespierre no doubt had its effect, but the crucial factor in bringing about the change was his absorption in William Godwin's famous treatise, *Enquiry concerning Political Justice*.[6] Though Wordsworth nowhere mentions *Political Justice* in *The Prelude*, the passage in which he describes his attempts to solve all moral problems by the light of "human Reason's naked self" is generally assumed to refer to that work.[7] *Political Justice*, which was published in February 1793 (nearly coincident with the outbreak of war), had an immediate and great impact upon the thinking of political liberals. "No work in our time," wrote William Hazlitt in *The Spirit of the Age*, "gave such a blow to the philosophical mind of the country." Wordsworth recaptures in *The Prelude* the glamour of its early enticement for him:

> What delight!
> How glorious! in self-knowledge and self-rule,
> To look through the frailties of the world,
> And . . .
> Build social freedom on its only basis,
> The freedom of the individual mind.

Wordsworth seems to have read *Political Justice* at the time of its publication and almost immediately to have fallen under its spell. At the outset, it is true, he "lent but a careless ear" to its "subtleties"; and in his "Letter to the Bishop of Llandaff," written in the spring of 1793, he surrendered himself only to those parts of *Political Justice* that fitted in—as so much of it did—with the "heart-bracing colloquies" of Beaupuy. In "The Female Vagrant," conceived and written in late summer of the same year, he stressed the broad humanitarian aspects of Godwin's creed, such as his protests against wealth and property, his sympathy with the outcasts of society, and his hatred of war. However, by the summer of 1794, a year later, Wordsworth was thinking of reform and revolution more closely in terms of the fundamental premises of Godwin's philosophy. Godwin severely condemned revolutions because "they suspend the wholesome advancement of science and confound the process of nature and reason." And reform, Godwin asserted, can only be effective when it advances step by step "with the illumination of our understanding."

An excellent example of Wordsworth's adoption of Godwin's premises can be found in his prospectus for "The Philanthropist, a Monthly Miscellany," which he expounds in June 1794 in a letter to his friend Mathews and which is crammed with ideas straight out of *Political Justice* couched in the language of its author. Among other things, Wordsworth wrote, "I recoil from the bare idea of a revolution"[8]—a striking reversal in the thinking of the man who just a year before in the "Letter to Llandaff" had offered arguments that could be used to justify the immediate overthrow of the British monarchy. Though Wordsworth was still an enemy of his country's institutions, he now saw through Godwin's eyes that the only way to end abuses was through education and the patient appeal to "reason."[9]

In the summer of 1794 Wordsworth's hopes for France were renewed when he heard by chance, while crossing the sands of the Leven estuary, that Robespierre was dead. He tells in *The Prelude* of his tremendous emotional

relief on hearing this news, being fully persuaded that once again the true
ideals of the revolution would be carried on. But when the French in 1795
"became oppressors in their turn" by ruthlessly invading other lands,
Wordsworth turned to Godwin's philosophy of pure reason as the only support left to save himself from chaos. His dependence on Godwinian rationalism, however, was of short duration. In a melancholy frame of mind
Wordsworth pushed his speculations forward

> till, demanding formal *proof,*
> And seeking it in everything, I lost
> All feeling of conviction, and, in fine,
> Sick, wearied out with contrarieties,
> Yielded up moral questions in despair.

From this quagmire of moral despair Wordsworth retreated to the firmer
ground of "mathematics and their clear and solid evidence." But he was in
dire need of further help, which by great good fortune was not long in
coming.

In the autumn of 1795 an old dream of Wordsworth and his sister
Dorothy to establish a home together was realized. Raisley Calvert, brother
to William Calvert, had died and left Wordsworth a legacy of £900; and
some new Bristol friends named Pinney had provided rent-free a hand-
somely furnished house in Dorset called Racedown Lodge. It was at
Racedown that Wordsworth came to terms with himself, cast off his despondency, and reentered the security of his true beliefs. His deliverance was
effected partly by a "return to Nature" and partly by the ministration of two
human agencies, Dorothy and Coleridge. Dorothy cheered and nourished
his spirit, reawakened his love of natural beauty, called out his compassion-
ate instincts for the poor and simple folk of Dorsetshire, and, best of all,
"preserved him still a poet." Coleridge, by his unstinting praise, gave
Wordsworth confidence in himself just when he most needed it. But the
road back was long, devious, and painful. Even the visitation of the "gentle
breeze" that roused his creative powers when he set out for Racedown from
Bristol and promised deliverance did not produce any startling poetic results. The first two months at Racedown were spent in revising and adding
to "Salisbury Plain." Then, after nearly a year of silence, Wordsworth began
his only drama, *The Borderers,* a five-act tragedy in blank verse.

The Borderers, a document in which can be read the story of
Wordsworth's convalescence at Racedown and his verdict upon Godwinian
ethics, reveals both an absorption in and a reaction to Godwin's doctrines. It

exposes the dangers of the intellect; at the same time, it upholds the validity and worth of benevolence. The story takes place in the thirteenth century in the borderland between England and Scotland, a region where there is no law "but what each man makes for himself." The action centers upon Oswald, whose apparent "motiveless malignity" is exposed. Some aspects of Wordsworth's moral crisis are revealed in the character of Oswald, but chiefly they are to be read in the actions and responses of his victim, Marmaduke. First, we need to know the story.

In his youth Oswald, a perfectly good man, "the pleasure of all hearts," went on a sea voyage to Syria. The crew persuades him, quite falsely, that the captain has initiated a foul conspiracy against his honor. In a mood of vengeful passion, Oswald insists that the captain be left on a barren island to starve to death; but he soon discovers that the crew has made him the agent of a plot to rid themselves of a master they hate. Some years later, in England, he meets Marmaduke, the "mirror of his youthful self," enjoying the love of a good woman. Oswald is driven to recreate his own fate in this counterpart of himself. He attaches himself, accordingly, to the company of borderers commanded by Marmaduke; and, having won his confidence and affection, he proceeds to poison his mind with suspicion.

Marmaduke hopes to marry Idonea, the beautiful and innocent daughter of old blind Herbert, once a baron but deprived arbitrarily of his rightful title and lands. But the subtle Oswald, by bribing a crazed vagrant woman, spreads the lie that Herbert bought her daughter Idonea and pretends she is his own and that he designs to pander Idonea to the lascivious Lord Clifford. By playing on Marmaduke's imagination with "a few swelling phrases, and a flash/Of truth, enough to dazzle and to blind," Oswald finally persuades Marmaduke in the absence of justice to murder the seemingly hypocritical old man.

In a dungeon "dark as the grave" Marmaduke is about to strike Herbert dead when a resemblance in the old man's face to Idonea's baffles him. He looks up to pray and, beholding through a crevice "a star twinkling above his head," cannot bring himself to kill him. Oswald is dismayed; but, with additional innuendos and pressures, he gets Marmaduke to resort to the superstition of an ordeal, whereby Marmaduke abandons Herbert on a desolate moor to starve. A shepherd, Eldred, whose character has been deceitfully sullied, discovers Herbert; but, since he cannot help the old man for fear of being suspected of foul play, he leaves him to die.

Oswald acclaims Marmaduke for throwing off the tyranny of custom and independently performing an act guided by the light of reason. Marmaduke, however, is filled with misgivings, which soon turn to anguish when he learns that Herbert is innocent. When Oswald's treachery is discovered, he is slain by the other borderers. Marmaduke, the once virtuous chief of the band, now crushed and filled with remorse, begins a solitary life of wandering penance.

Despite the romance elements in the plot, *The Borderers* is preeminently a psychological drama and consequently goes well beyond the philosophy of William Godwin. The play centers on the psychology of one character, Oswald, and even more narrowly on what Wordsworth called his "apparently motiveless crime," his seduction of the protagonist, Marmaduke, into committing murder.

A good deal has been written about this play; scholars have discussed its possible Gothic sources, the possible influence of Wordsworth's own involvement in the French Revolution and his later moral crisis, and especially the alleged similarity of Oswald to Shakespeare's Iago. This latter issue, however, has been put to rest by the revelation of the substantial differences between the two characters.[10]

Wordsworth himself wrote an essay of almost two thousand words on the character of Oswald, as well as a short preface when the play was published in 1842 and a more general brief note dictated to Isabella Fenwick in 1843.[11] Wordsworth's own views are clearly the best place to start in examining the play, although in these circumstances it is always necessary to look beyond the writer's intentions to his actual accomplishment. In this case, the two are the same, with but few reservations.

According to Wordsworth, Oswald was created "to shew the dangerous use which may be made of reason when a man has committed a great crime" and to dramatize the application of "moral sentiments . . . to vicious purposes." Morality is clearly mixed with the psychology, resulting in considerable complexity. In the case of both Oswald and Marmaduke, the "murders" they commit are complicated by the extenuating circumstances of their having been tricked by others into committing the crimes, to the point of there being no crime at all. Wordsworth has further complicated the issue by placing both men in circumstances beyond the law where moral decisions must nevertheless be made. Only Oswald's betrayal of Marmaduke into killing Clifford is clearly evil and thus constitutes the central action of the play.

Oswald is not a fundamentally evil man, as has been claimed, but he does have fundamental weaknesses—pride and the "love of distinction" (or vanity)—that come into play given the right situations. He is also described by Wordsworth as restless and devoid of benevolence. The situation that sets this volatile mixture in motion is the murder of the sea captain that occurs before the play opens and that is not itself, I have already argued, an evil act.

The process of Oswald's moral deterioration following this act is described similarly in Wordsworth's essay and in the play. He loses his influence with the crew that tricked him and so becomes disgusted and misanthropic. He withdraws and reexamines morality, ending in moral skepticism and finally in cynicism. On returning to the world, he becomes more pragmatic, committing evil deeds but continuing his speculations— this combination of the contemplative and the active giving depth to his characterization. He resorts to rationalizations to justify himself, demonstrating just the perversion of reason Wordsworth set out to show.

Oswald's "apparently motiveless crime" of reducing Marmaduke to murder did in fact have at least two motives that are given in both the play and the essay: Marmaduke had saved Oswald's life, and "gratitude's a heavy burden/To a proud soul"; and Marmaduke had been chosen over Oswald as leader of the band, making Oswald envious and resentful. Yet these were not considered sufficient motives either by Wordsworth or by his critics.

Wordsworth offers four more considerations that are both subtle and paradoxical to make the motivation more credible. The nonexistence of a motive for someone like Oswald who dotes on strangeness can itself be a motive; Oswald hates Marmaduke the more because he knows he shouldn't; the dissatisfied mind tends to seek more evil, not less; and every new evil deed defies remorse the more. Wordsworth, moreover, adds at the end of his essay that trivial motives behind serious crimes are often forgotten, and he points out the contortions the evil mind is capable of, of which the normal mind is unaware.

Oswald is a complex character; he is certainly more than the innately evil man that he is sometimes taken to be and that would be considerably less interesting. He is a man who commits evil because of a weak character worked upon by psychological forces once the proper situations materialize. Oswald is at least a limited success, for he does show the complicated process by which morality is perverted by reason.

As a piece of drama, however, *The Borderers* has little to commend it. Coleridge thought it "absolutely wonderful," but it was rejected as unfit for the stage, and readers have since found it rather dull. It is interesting as Wordsworth's first prolonged attempt at blank verse and as revealing his patent indebtedness to Shakespeare in the Iago-like character of Oswald and in borrowings from *Macbeth, Lear,* and *Hamlet.* Wordsworth takes over the entire machinery of Gothic romance in the suspenseful terror of the murder scenes; and, in the character of the villain-hero Oswald, he owes much to the prideful tyrants of Mrs. Ann Radcliffe and Friedrich Schiller.

But Wordsworth was not simply reproducing the ruthlessness of fictional characters in his drama. He also had before his eyes the sinister figures of Robespierre, Jean Paul Marat, and their kind, who wrought havoc upon human happiness. They are the flesh-and-blood counterparts of Oswald, as Wordsworth himself afterward testified in the short preface of 1842: "During my long residence in France, while the Revolution was rapidly advancing to its extreme of wickedness, I had frequent opportunities of being an eye-witness of this process [i.e., the progressive hardening of the heart], and it was while that knowledge was fresh upon my memory, that the Tragedy of 'The Borderers' was written."

Poet of the Human Heart: "The Old Cumberland Beggar" and "The Ruined Cottage"

By the time Wordsworth finished *The Borderers,* he had resolved the inner discords that had plagued him since his return from France. Through the stimulating companionship of Dorothy he had rediscovered nature's healing power and was prepared to fuse his renewed love of nature with a new orientation to society. He was ready to celebrate in his poetry those aspects of nature and humanity most likely to encourage the benevolent affections. The first poem embodying his new vision of man and nature was "The Old Cumberland Beggar," completed at Racedown in 1797. Its setting is the Lake District, and the beggar is one of that fraternity the poet remembered from his boyhood who "confined themselves to a stated round in their neighbourhoods" and were sure of alms at various houses.

Wordsworth made the old man the subject of a poem as a protest against the "political economists" who at that time were prosecuting a "war upon mendicity in all its forms." The politicians saw beggary as a social nuisance, but Wordsworth did not want to see the state push the beggars off the roads into the "HOUSE, misnamed INDUSTRY." He was dead set against workhouses as a cure for unemployment, places that in most cases were comfortless asylums for the poor and aged. Wordsworth made his plea to let the old beggar remain free to live and die "in the eye of Nature." His person is hallowed by his nearness to nature and precious because his helplessness keeps alive the compassion of man. The horseman stops to place the proffered coin safely within the old man's hat; she who tends the tollgate stops her work when she sees the aged beggar coming and lifts the latch for him; the boisterous postboy turns his wheels aside and passes gently by: "Where'er the aged Beggar takes his rounds,/The mild necessity of use compels/To acts of love." The country folk come to think of the beggar as a constituent part of their lives. But Wordsworth goes even beyond the common response to underscore the benevolent interrelationship of all creation:

> 'Tis Nature's law
> That none, the meanest of created things,
> Of forms created the most vile and brute,
> The dullest or more noxious, should exist
> Divorced from good—a spirit and pulse of good,
> A life and soul, to every mode of being
> Inseparably linked.

Yet it is the human community that remains the central concern of the poem; the beggar binds together the villagers through their charity toward him, through the warm feeling that results—"the after-joy/That reason cherishes"—a feeling that today is frowned upon, oddly enough, as besmirching one's altruism.

Charles Lamb complained that there was too much lecturing in the poem. But, if this is so, there is also in the descriptive parts an awareness of suffering among the aged that was new in poetry, at least since Shakespeare. And the beggar seems to hold within him, as Wordsworth's solitaries so often do, the "secret of inscrutable dignity." As John F. Danby says, "He has endured the accidents of experience past the point at which experience has any further power to give or to take away."[12] The old beggar "is by nature led/To peace so perfect that the young behold/With envy, what the Old Man hardly feels." In this regard, he becomes something more than a social problem: he is an archetype of the inherent value of human personality, a precious proof that "all of us have one human heart."

An even better poem than "The Old Cumberland Beggar" embodying Wordsworth's new humanitarianism, if not a more light-hearted one, is "The Ruined Cottage."[13] The story is a simple one. The cottage of the title had recently been inhabited by a weaver and his wife and their two children. Their married life had begun in happiness, but became stricken by successive seasons of blighted harvests and by the plague of war. Margaret struggled through those calamitous years with cheerful hope until Robert, her husband, fell ill of a fever. This costly illness, which consumed their small savings, was followed by a prolonged period in which Robert could find no work. In despair, he joined a troop of soldiers going to a foreign land. Margaret, left alone, tried to keep up hope; but, as time passed and she heard no tidings of her husband, her spirits drooped; she became listless and negligent. The cottage lost its neatness; weeds defaced the hardened soil of the garden; her baby died. For five long years she lingered alone in the cottage, which from neglect sank into decay; at last, she became ill from exposure and died.

The narrative of "The Ruined Cottage" bears some resemblance to that of the female vagrant in "Guilt and Sorrow," but the story is told without bitterness and with a new objectivity. This objectivity is aided by the poet's use of a narrator, a "Pedlar" (later to become the Wanderer of *The Excursion*), and by setting the story in an earlier time. Much of the power of "The Ruined Cottage" comes from the skillful handling of the significant detail through which the poet reveals the relentless grinding down of Robert and Margaret—the blighted harvests, the prolonged and costly illness, the enforced idleness, war, and desertion.

The pedlar on his visits to the cottage observes the changes that have taken place in his absence. The border tufts have invaded the garden paths they used to deck; a toadstool has sprung up by the broken arbor. Through these details and many similar ones simply reported by the pedlar, Wordsworth typifies the process of ruin that has overtaken everything human and man-made in the poem. The details are symbolic and, as such, offer insight into Margaret's problem and character. The outward manifestations of decay are the signs of inner psychological disintegration.

Without her husband, Margaret struggles hopelessly for survival. Her grief is compulsive and inconsolable. For five tedious years "she lingered on in unquiet widowhood," "a sore heart-wasting." From the broken arbor, if a dog passed by, she would quit the shade and look abroad. Whenever a discharged soldier or a mendicant sailor passed the cottage, or a stranger horseman came by the roadside gate, with faltering voice she would question him, still hoping to learn something of her husband's fate. The poem closes with lines of acute poignancy:

> Meanwhile her poor hut
> Sank to decay, for he was gone, whose hand
> At the first nippings of October frost
> Closed up each chink, and with fresh bands of straw
> Chequered the green-grown thatch. And so she lived

Through the long winter, reckless and alone;
Till this reft house, by frost, and thaw, and rain
Was sapped, and, when she slept, the nightly damps
Did chill her breast, and in the stormy day
Her tattered clothes were ruffled by the wind
Even at the side of her own fire. Yet still
She loved this wretched spot, nor would for worlds
Have parted hence, and still that length of road
And this rude bench one torturing hope endeared,
Fast rooted at her heart; and here, my friend,
In sickness she remained, and here she died,
Last human tenant of these ruined walls.

In "The Ruined Cottage" Wordsworth ceased to be a social reformer; he became a poet of the human heart. Believing now that attacks on the social order were likely to result in more harm than good, he was determined "to stress in his poetry the serene rather than the turbulent in nature, the good rather than the evil in common humanity."[14] Accordingly, he united in these poems his love of nature with a belief in a benevolent necessity for the whole of society. Midway in "The Ruined Cottage" the pedlar explains to the poet, his listener, that it would be wantonness to take pleasure in recounting the sufferings of Margaret if there were not "often found/In mournful thoughts, and always might be found,/A power to virtue friendly." In the original manuscript Wordsworth closed the poem with a long reflective argument (afterward incorporated into *The Excursion*, book 4) in which he tells how, by degrees, the painful story of Margaret became softened in his thoughts until he felt "a holy tenderness pervade his frame." So it was providentially meant that, out of all human experiences, whether of suffering or of joy, man's being should be oriented to moral goodness:

Thus deeply drinking in the soul of things
We shall be wise perforce, and we shall move
From strict necessity along the path
Of order and of good.

"The Ruined Cottage" marks a manifest advance in Wordsworth's poetic power as well as in his social attitude. He makes no use of terror or Gothic trappings to jack up an emotional response. He does not exaggerate, nor deplore, nor condemn; and at no point does he intrude a grudge against society. Instead of resentment toward the oppressors of the poor (such as he had felt in his revolutionary days), he awakens by simple, unadorned statements sympathy and love for the gentle Margaret. With this remarkably fine poem, Wordsworth's formative years as a poet ended. He entered at last into his true heritage.

Chapter Two
Lyrical Ballads, 1798

Two Poets Join Forces and *Lyrical Ballads* Is Born

On a memorable day at Racedown in June 1797, Wordsworth recited "The Ruined Cottage" to Coleridge, who hailed it "the finest poem in our language, comparing it with any of the same or similar length."[1] Coleridge's admiration for his new friend, as well as for his friend's poetry, was unbounded. In a letter to Joseph Cottle, he spoke of Wordsworth with heartfelt sincerity as "the greatest man I ever knew."[2] Wordsworth was equally drawn to Coleridge, for each discovered in the other the fulfillment of an immediate need. Coleridge found in Wordsworth a friend who recognized his genius and who offered a steady hand to direct it. In return, besides the kindling warmth of unstinted admiration, Coleridge gave to Wordsworth the vast resources of his fertilizing intellect. "He was most wonderful," Wordsworth wrote long afterward, "in the power he possessed of throwing out in profusion grand central truths from which might be evolved the most comprehensive systems."[3]

Within a month of Coleridge's visit, the Racedown household was broken up; William and Dorothy, in order to be near Coleridge, settled at Alfoxden, a lovely Queen Anne mansion about three miles from Coleridge's cottage at Nether Stowey. During the momentous year that was to follow, from July 1797 to July 1798, the two friends enjoyed daily companionship and almost constant exaltation of spirits. With the fervor of high-minded youth, they talked of making the world better through their poetry. They hoped in that time of national crisis and pessimism to bring to men, disillusioned by the French Revolutionary idea, the secret they had discovered of the principle of joy in the universe. They would preach no political or social reform; and, in order to reach men, they would cast out of their writing all poetic diction and return to directness, sincerity, and basic human emotions. The older writers and the traditional ballads would be their models.

To realize their dreams, the two poets tried several times to collaborate, but never with success. From one of these attempts, however, was born the idea of *Lyrical Ballads*. Late in the afternoon of 13 November, 1797,

William, Dorothy, and Coleridge began a walking trip to the Valley of Stones near Lynmouth. To defray the modest expenses of their journey, they planned to compose a ballad to be sold to the *New Monthly Magazine*. In the course of their walk that evening, they began together the composition of "The Ancient Mariner" to which Wordsworth, as he said, "made several trifling contributions." As they continued to compose that same evening, however, their manners proved so widely different that Wordsworth withdrew from the undertaking. The practical difficulties of collaboration brought to light the fundamental differences in their mental operations, and they began to talk of a volume of poems, to which both would contribute, but with each working in his own manner. Coleridge gives a graphic account twenty years later in his *Biographia Literaria,* chapter 14, of the division of labor between them:

The thought suggested itself (to which of us I do not recollect) that a series of poems might be composed of two sorts. In the one, the incidents and agents were to be, in part at least, supernatural; and the excellence aimed at was to consist in the interesting of the affections by the dramatic truth of such emotions, as would naturally accompany such situations, supposing them real. . . . For the second class, subjects were to be chosen from ordinary life; the characters and incidents were to be such as will be found in every village and its vicinity, where there is a meditative and feeling mind to seek after them, or to notice them, when they present themselves.

In this idea originated the plan of *Lyrical Ballads,* in which it was agreed that my endeavours should be directed to persons and characters supernatural, or at least romantic; yet so as to transfer from our inward nature a human interest . . . sufficient to procure for these shadows of imagination that willing suspension of disbelief for the moment, which constitutes poetic faith. Mr. Wordsworth, on the other hand, was to propose to himself as his object, to give the charm of novelty to things of every day, and to excite a feeling analogous to the supernatural, by awakening the mind's attention from the lethargy of custom, and directing it to the loveliness and wonders of the world before us.

[Both of them were to observe] the two cardinal points of poetry, the power of exciting the sympathy of the reader by a faithful adherence to the truth of nature, and the power of giving the interest of novelty by the modifying colours of imagination.

In March 1798, Coleridge put the finishing touches to "The Rime of the Ancient Mariner," which was given first place in the new volume. He began "Christabel" with high hopes, but he got through only part 1 that spring and never finished it. Wordsworth, until the first week of March, was engaged entirely in blank-verse composition; but, from early March to May

1798, a flood tide of inspiration resulted in a number of poems written expressly for the projected volume with the theory in mind. Scholars know, incidentally, from a letter written to James Tobin on 6 March that the theory was not created afterward merely to justify the poems. Theory and poetry went hand in hand. During the summer the offerings of each poet deemed suitable for the new volume were gathered together and taken to Joseph Cottle of Bristol for publication. That glorious afterthought, "Tintern Abbey," written in September, was added later to the other pieces already prepared for the press. The joint collection was entitled *Lyrical Ballads, with a Few Other Poems* and was provided with a short "Advertisement" written by Wordsworth.

The Intention and Originality of the New Poetry

In his preamble Wordsworth recorded the chief points of the new poetic theory and sought to disarm readers against prejudging the experimental poems written under it. He reminds his readers that the materials of poetry are "to be found in every subject which can interest the human mind." He states that the majority of the poems in the volume are to be considered as experiments. "They were written," he says, "chiefly with a view to ascertain how far the language of conversation in the middle and lower classes of society is adapted to the purposes of poetic pleasure." What Wordsworth does not say, but what one learns from the Preface to *Lyrical Ballads*, 1800, written at length to defend them (of which more later), is that he wanted to represent life concretely in his poetry—to penetrate the "lethargy of custom" and make people feel anew the primal impulses common to all mankind.

To achieve this result, Wordsworth concentrated on the emotion to be aroused by the subject of the poem and not on the subject itself; as he says in the 1800 Preface, "The feeling therein developed gives importance to the action and situation and not the action and situation to the feeling." He intended that the emotion aroused by his poems would be so powerful and of such a kind that it would reveal, as with a religious force, the workings of the human heart. By this means he hoped also to awaken and spread abroad (a wish close to his heart) a humanitarian attitude toward those born to "a poor and humble lot."

There is no trace of the talks between the two poets that resulted in the title *Lyrical Ballads;* however, they have left sufficient evidence to permit us to interpret their intended meaning. Both of them were great admirers of Bishop Percy's collection of traditional ballads, *Reliques of Ancient Poetry* (published in 1765), and Wordsworth declared in his Preface of 1815 that

English poetry had been "absolutely redeemed by it." There were also contemporary broadside ballads hawked in the streets, such as "Babes in the Wood," which Wordsworth would have heard in London and which very well could have served him as models for such pieces as "Goody Blake and Harry Gill." He wrote to Francis Wrangham that some of his poems had been written with a view to their eventual circulation as broadsides and so, perhaps, to their supplanting the halfpenny ballads of the time; they were "flowers and useful herbs to take the place of weeds."[4] Also in popular favor at that time were the translations of German ballad imitations, especially G. A. Bürger's "Lenore" and "Die wilde Jäger." And there were imitations of all these ballads in the magazines, newspapers, and pamphlets in which current poetry appeared. But in their title *Lyrical Ballads* Wordsworth and Coleridge chiefly had in mind Percy's folk ballads. In them a tragic story is narrated. On the other hand, in a lyric poem the essence is a heightened emotion. That is why "lyrical" comes into the title, for in their ballads the emphasis is not on the story or the dramatic events but on the emotions embodied in the story. The stories are reduced to their pathetic human essentials; the heartrending situations are actualized. Because of the feeling, the lyrical element, one must accept the story, willingly suspend disbelief in the supernatural happenings of "The Ancient Mariner," or be interested in such trivialities of adventure as occur in "The Idiot Boy."

Lyrical Ballads was published anonymously by J. and A. Arch, London (Cottle at the last minute having transferred his copyright), in October 1798. Of the twenty-three poems in the volume, four are by Coleridge, including, besides "The Ancient Mariner," a conversation piece in blank verse entitled "The Nightingale" and two extracts from his tragedy *Osorio*, "The Foster Mother's Tale" and "The Dungeon." Of Coleridge's contributions, only "The Ancient Mariner" was written to fulfill his assignment in the new poetic theory. However, the majority of Wordsworth's contributions, which total nineteen, were written expressly for the projected volume with the theory in mind. Those not involving the theory, apart from "Tintern Abbey," which Wordsworth himself says was composed in the loftier and impassioned strain of the ode, were poems written before 1797—"Lines Left upon a Seat in a Yew-tree," "The Female Vagrant," "Lines written near Richmond," "The Convict," and "The Old Man Travelling"—none of which show any trace of ballad literature.

Eleven of the other poems, in a variety of ways, are the real experiment wherein Wordsworth attempts to coordinate the artless art of the ballad with his own observation of the psychological processes underlying the lives of simple men.[5] The originality of Wordsworth's contributions to *Lyrical*

Ballads was in the psychological mode and power of the poems and in their language rather than in their subject matter. His figures, settings, and themes were common-places in the magazine poetry of the day;[6] but no other poet brought to them such an eye for precise observation, such an ear for the vernacular, or such a heart and mind for probing deeply the essentials of man's being.

Wordsworth turned his back on his personal life and, as has been said, "made something of a strenuous voyage of discovery—a sort of arctic expedition—into a region where life was reduced to its elements, the outward trappings at their simplest."[7] His intention above all in *Lyrical Ballads,* as he stated in the 1800 Preface, was to make incidents and situations chosen from common life "interesting by tracing in them . . . the primary laws of our nature: chiefly, as far as regards the manner in which we associate ideas in a state of excitement." What he did was to turn tragic subjects into psychological studies so that the feeling developed could give importance to the action.

To support his aim, Wordsworth deliberately imitated the speech of the lower classes, purified, of course, of all annoying peculiarities of vocabulary and syntax. He sometimes employed the mannerisms of popular ballads, such as the repetition of pronouns after a substantive ("The doctor *he* has made him wait") or reduplication in the predicate to reveal an inattentive mind ("*It* stands erect, *this aged thorn*"). Sometimes he tried to suggest the naïveté of folk ballads through language and rhythms that were unsophisticated to the point of doggerel. There were gains and losses from Wordsworth's conscious attempt to use "the language of the middle and lower classes for the purposes of poetic pleasure." Yet, overall, the newness of style and the simplicity of language (despite its occasional crudeness) give an impression of poetry operating in a new dimension of freshness and depth.

On one level, Wordsworth's experiment involved poetic diction; but, at a deeper level, *Lyrical Ballads* is an experiment in modes of dramatic technique.[8] In order to mask his own passion and to identify himself with the passions that stirred his characters, Wordsworth used dramatic self-projection. Of the eleven experimental poems, nine are dramatic or semidramatic in form. In these he used a variety of methods, picking up and laying down his masks. Sometimes he is the narrator, sometimes the characters involved, and sometimes the poet himself. By changing the voice, he can step from one frame to another and back again: the storyteller, story, and poet-manipulator are reciprocally and dramatically related. By using all the devices of language, meter, and dramatic modes available to him as a poet, he hoped to convey passion to readers not accustomed to sympathizing with men in the lower levels of society whose manner and language differed from their own.

"The Thorn"

"The Thorn" carries out Wordsworth's avowed intention to trace in situations of common life "the primary laws of our nature." Like Coleridge's "The Ancient Mariner" and his own *Peter Bell* and "Goody Blake and Harry Gill," the poem is a study in mental pathology. In its own fashion, it illustrates the tremendous effect upon the imagination of a painful idea vividly impressed upon the mind. It grew out of Wordsworth's excited notice of a stunted thorn tree, which, under the unusual aspects of mist and rain, was revealed to him with visionary impressiveness. He wanted to produce on other minds the effect that the "poetry of nature" had produced on his mind.

To commemorate his vision, he attached a tragic story to the scene; and he chose as a medium of communication to the reader a simple narrator in the person of a loquacious, retired sea captain. Wordsworth had a surprisingly specific narrator in mind; and, in a long note to the poem in 1800, he spelled out in detail his character and mental habits. He is an important link to the poem but not an end in himself. As Wordsworth describes him, he is credulous and talkative from indolence, prone to superstition, slow of faculties and deep in feelings, and has a modest endowment of imagination. He is represented as sharing his thoughts with a simple villager of less sensitivity than his own. His language is folk-oriented, watered down by clichés, and encumbered with almost obsessive repetitions. But he is an honest witness. For all the self-imposed fetters under which Wordsworth labors, he handles his materials with artistic sophistication and with a high degree of effectiveness.

The narrator begins in a matter-of-fact, repetitious manner by describing the thorn tree as an "aged" and "a wretched thing" encumbered with mosses. It becomes for the reader an emblem of the human story of Martha Ray in her misery; to the villagers, as represented by the mariner, it is an emblem of the crime of child murder. The poem continues in the same flat, repetitious language with a description of the muddy pond, then in more fanciful language presents a beauteous hill of moss and a woman who often sits beside it:

> A Woman in a scarlet cloak,
> And to herself she cries,

"Oh misery! oh misery!
Oh woe is me! oh misery!"

The near-banal repetitions used by the narrator in describing the thorn and
the pond thwart the reader's sympathetic response and hold it in abeyance.
But, when the plaintive cry of the lonely woman is repeated, the reader's
emotions are released. To reinforce and sustain them, Wordsworth's own
passion and beauty of language break through in the next stanza:

> At all times of the day and night
> This wretched Woman thither goes;
> And she is known to every star,
> And every wind that blows;
> And there beside the Thorn she sits
> When the blue day-light's in the skies,
> And when the whirlwind's on the hill,
> Or frosty air is keen and still,
> And to herself she cries,
> "Oh misery! oh misery!
> Oh woe is me! oh misery!"

The proper conditions have now been established for the mariner to tell
the poor woman's story as he has been able to piece it together. Some two
and twenty years ago Martha Ray gave her company to Stephen Hill, who
promised to marry her. But Stephen forsook her, though she was carrying
his child, and married another. On that woeful day she lost her reason, but
a villager claims her reason was restored just before her child was born. No
one ever knew when or where Martha Ray gave birth to the child; but
about that time some remember that she often climbed up the mountain
and that at night, when the wind blew, cries were heard coming from the
mountain peak. Some say they were living voices; others swear they were
voices of the dead.

After the narrator has finished his story, he tells how he chanced one
day in a windy rainstorm to come across Martha Ray in a scarlet cloak sitting beside the old thorn. He did not speak, but he heard her cry, "Oh
misery! Oh misery!" At this point, to heighten the coloring of imagination,
Wordsworth invokes village superstitions that touch the incident with
mystery and awe. Some say she strangled or drowned her baby and buried
it beneath the hill of moss. Some say the scarlet moss is red from the infant's blood. And some say

> if to the pond you go,
> And fix on it a steady view,
> The shadow of a babe you trace,
> A baby and a baby's face,
> And that it looks at you.

At the end, attention is focused upon the thorn bound with the heavy tufts of moss that strive to drag it to the ground; and the poem closes with the repeated cries of Martha Ray reverberating in the reader's consciousness.

How successful, one may ask, was Wordsworth in adopting his new poetical theories in "The Thorn"? Coleridge objected to "a daring humbleness of Language and Versification, and a strict adherence to matter of fact, even to prolixity." He thought it was not possible "to imitate truly a dull and garrulous discourser, without repeating the effects of dullness and garrulity." Wordsworth made significant changes after Coleridge's criticism; but, in refining the narrator's language, the poet makes him less dramatically convincing. Wordsworth was more nearly right in the first rendering, for the narrator's very irrelevancies and redundancies force the reader to take in his full story's span and, after the reader's mind has been freed from them, to feel the shock of man's inhumanity to man. A strong feeling of compassion survives at the end. "The Thorn" misses by a narrow margin being one of Wordsworth's great poems.

"The Idiot Boy"

"The Idiot Boy" offered a sharper challenge to current taste than any other poem in *Lyrical Ballads*. It was criticized and ridiculed on all sides, yet the poem always remained one of Wordsworth's favorites. He composed it with great glee almost extempore. It is a poem of mixed modes, being at once poignantly real and comically absurd. On the comic side, it is essentially a rustic mock-epic including a life-and-death issue, the last chance of success depending upon the person least likely to succeed, frantic search and rescue of the rescuer, and finally the happy resolution of everyone's afflictions. Wordsworth, who meant for the reader to enjoy the bathos of the adventure, supports the comic mood with empty phrases and feminine rhymes: "fiddle-faddle—saddle"; "shocked her—doctor."

The whole action is a kind of burlesque of knight-errantry. The champion to the rescue is Johnny Foy, the Idiot Boy. The affectionate mother of the Idiot Boy is Betty Foy, neighbor to Old Susan Gale, who lives alone. One clear March night, when the moon is up and the owls are shouting,

Susan Gale falls painfully ill. There is none within a mile around to help, and Betty cannot leave her alone. So Betty mounts her idiot boy upon a pony and excitedly tells him—directions repeated over and over—to fetch the doctor in the village. Betty proudly watches her idiot boy depart, but one can guess that he will not go far upon the right way; for he is mounted on "a horse that thinks/And when he thinks, his pace is slack." Poor Susan and Betty wait and wait until past midnight for the doctor and his guide. When her anxiety for Johnny can no longer be withstood— "he is but half-wise"—she leaves Susan to search for him. She hastens to the village and there rouses the doctor, who sleepily and grumblingly declares he has seen nothing of Johnny. Poor Betty is so overcome with worry over her idiot boy that she completely forgets to send the doctor to Old Susan Gale. It is now three o'clock, and Betty has lost all hope. Suddenly the thought strikes her that the pony, "who is mild and good," has perhaps carried Johnny along the dell to the family woodlot.

And what has Johnny been doing all this time? Perhaps, says the narrator, giving his fancy reign, he is riding up the cliffs and peaks to lay his hands upon a star; perhaps, like Don Quixote (for the idiot was a "natural" like La Mancha's knight), he's hunting sheep, "A fierce and dreadful hunter he!" But, in truth, Johnny, though near the thunderous waterfall, is just sitting upright upon his mount as the pony feeds upon the grass. Good Betty Foy, when she sees him whom she loves, screams with delight; and, in her eagerness to embrace him (Wordsworth describes her action with a touch of slapstick), she almost overturns the horse. Alive with joy, she kisses and kisses again her idiot boy and tells him to never mind the doctor. Meanwhile, poor old Susan, beset by fears over what has happened to Betty and her idiot boy, rises from her bed as if cured by magic. The three are happily reunited and Johnny, when asked by Betty where he had been,

> Made answer, like a traveller bold,
> (His very words I give to you,)
> "The cocks did crow to-whoo, to-whoo,
> And the sun did shine so cold!"
> —Thus answered Johnny in his glory,
> And that was all his travel's story. ·

The action of Wordsworth's mock-heroic is dramatically paced and well timed; the rattling comic tempo never lets up. The tone is "beautifully mock-solemn yet indulgently ready with its sympathy."[9] The reader is called upon for tenderness yet is not asked to surrender his identity. Wordsworth as narrator makes the reader aware of his masks. He assumes a colloquial personality and addresses intermittent, half-jocular remarks to his muse, to the reader, and to the characters in his tale. The result is an irony that permits the reader to sympathize with the anguished passion of Betty Foy at the same time that it allows for an awareness of the exuberant delight of the poet's play of mind and turns of emotion.

Because of Wordsworth's levity of style, a derisive public mistook his basic purpose, which was to illustrate the depth of a mother's love lavished upon an object repellent to others. Coleridge, who attacked "The Idiot Boy," charged that the author had not "taken sufficient care to preclude from the reader's fancy the disgusting images of *ordinary morbid idiocy*" and that he had, as a result, produced a "laughable burlesque on the blindness of anile dotage."[10] John Wilson, a young fan who later became editor of *Blackwood's*, wrote and frankly confessed his inability to care for the poem: "I admire the talents of the *artist*, the *picture* disgusts me inexpressibly."

Wordsworth wrote a spirited rejoinder to Wilson reproaching him and others for a false delicacy that showed "a certain want of comprehensiveness in thinking and feeling." For himself, he said, he often applied to idiots "that sublime expression of Scripture, that their life is hidden with God." Without condescension or moralizing, Wordsworth got right inside his characters and traced for his readers' edification the love which gives freely and without thought of any reward. Unfortunately, the reading public has not yet accepted Wordsworth's poem on the terms in which it was offered.

Peter Bell

Like "The Thorn" and "The Idiot Boy," *Peter Bell* was originally intended to be one of Wordsworth's experimental poems in *Lyrical Ballads;* but it was too long for inclusion and was withheld from publication until 1819. When it did appear, it was parodied and ridiculed on all sides, though it was called by Coleridge "most wonderful and admirable." Coleridge's tribute is the more significant because he knew that *Peter Bell* was his friend's rival to "The Ancient Mariner." As Wordsworth explained in his prefatory letter to Southey, dated 7 April 1819, *Peter Bell* was "composed under a belief that the imagination not only does not require for its exercise the intervention of supernatural agency, but that, though such agency be excluded, the faculty may be called forth as imperiously, and for kindred results of pleasure, by incidents within the compass of poetic probability, in the humblest departments of daily life."

Precisely as in "The Ancient Mariner," Wordsworth's poem tells of the wanton cruelty of a man toward an animal and of the release of the man from the consequences of his crime through a gush of pity. But, whereas in "The Ancient Mariner" the consequences are magical, the sinner in *Peter Bell* is frightened into becoming "a good and honest man" by a mental process that is strictly psychological—by tricks of moonlight, echoes of an ass's bray, the cry of a boy searching for his dead father, a withered leaf, some Methodist hymn singers, and finally a weeping woman. The poem is one of Wordsworth's studies of the workings of the human mind, and it is a testament to his central faith that nature, even in the humblest departments of daily life, is capable of influencing for good even one of her more rebellious and insensitive children.

Though the theme of *Peter Bell* is highly serious, its form and treatment are comic. Wordsworth uses light tetrameter stanzas and a folksy diction appropriate to the narrator in his role as provincial poet. In the prologue, the poet asks to be let down among his simple neighbors to tell a tale of "The common growth of mother-earth." In all three parts of the poem, the language is pitched on the colloquial level, and the verses are spun out with bathetic wordiness. In no other poem by Wordsworth is the diction so daringly common-place and the humor so blatantly realistic. Much of the humor was progressively toned down in succeeding revisions, but much of the comic earthiness remains in the poem to delight appreciative readers or to feed the spleen of the parodists.

The hero of the story is Peter Bell, a wild rover such as Wordsworth had walked with along the river Wye. A potter by trade, he has for more than thirty years been living in the open air and traveling in sight of the grand and the beautiful. But he was brutal, immoral, and insensitive. Nature never could find the way into his heart: "A primrose by a river's brim/A yellow primrose was to him,/And it was nothing more." However, the terrors he experiences one beautiful moonlight night open the way to his regeneration.

On that night in November, Peter, while trudging along all alone beside the river Swale, took a path that promised to shorten his way. The path leads him to a quarry and, beyond it, to a meadow where he discovers a solitary ass with his head hanging over a stream. In his pique over missing his way, Peter determines to steal the ass. Accordingly, he leaps upon the creature's back, kicks him, and wildly jerks on the halter; but the ass will not budge. Wordsworth confesses that "he took delight in the habits, odd tricks, and physiognomy of the asses that roamed the Alfoxden woods." At this point in the action, he interjects a comical observation. Peter, fearful of being discovered in his theft, leaps from the back of the ass and cautiously looks around him. All is silent far and near—"Only the Ass, with motion dull,/Upon the pivot of his skull/Turns round his long left ear."

Peter now raises his staff and staggers the "patient, uncomplaining beast" with a cruel blow. The ass drops gently upon his knees; falls and lies upon the river's bank; and, as he does so, turns a reproachful look upon Peter. The hardhearted rover mercilessly beats the helpless creature until he lies still as death. With a curse Peter declares he will fling him into the river. Whereupon the ass sends forth a clamorous bray; and, as Peter turns to his demonic work, the ass again more ruefully lengthens out "The hard dry see-saw of his horrible bray!" A strange fear seizes Peter; he drops his staff, bends over the water, and imagines that he sees in its depths strange sights: Is it a gallows, a coffin, or a shroud? Is it a grisly idol, imp, or fiend? What he sees is a dead man's face seen through the water by moonlight. Astonishment and fear seize Peter; he looks fascinated—"he cannot choose but look"; then, with a frightful shriek, he falls back into a dead faint. The process of inward change has begun, though at first the only manifestations are terror.

Peter at length recovers from his swoon; and, encouraged by the ass, who stands beside him, he probes the stream until he dislodges and hauls to shore the drowned master over whom the ass had kept watch without food for four days. Strange pity surges through the heart of Peter, and he vows to do whatever the ass would have him do. He mounts upon the creature's back (the mounting on the ass is for Peter what his blessing of the water snakes had been for the Ancient Mariner) and is carried toward the master's home; but he is confronted on the way with a series of "severe interventions" that best serve nature's own aims. Near the quarry's mouth a strange, piercing cry strikes Peter's ear, the likes of which he has never heard. His fear is quickened by the wild, fantastic shadows of the quarry rocks and even by the rustling of a withered leaf. When he sees the bloody wound he had inflicted on the ass's head, a ghostly agony passes through his brain. An underground explosion in the mine beneath him adds to his terror.

But, of all these sights and sounds, one is of special importance; for it coalesces with an important memory. A ruined chapel they pass reminds him of a similar scene in Fifeshire, where he married his sixth wife, a mere girl of sixteen. The scene, with its associated memories, turns him adrift into the past. Wordsworth now calls upon "Spirits of the Mind" (such ministrants as he himself in boyhood had felt in darkness or stormy night) to show their empire over the heart of Peter Bell. Peter has the shocking experience of seeing a vision of himself, "an unsubstantial creature," "not four yards from the broad highway"; and "stretched beneath the furze" is his poor Highland child-wife, the victim of his wickedness, dying there before him. A grievous contrition seizes Peter, which is shortly thereafter confirmed by the voice of a Methodist preacher crying aloud from a tabernacle, "Repent! repent!" When the ass leads the way to his owner's home, the widow piteously questions Peter about her dead husband; and, when the miner's orphaned boy returns and lovingly greets the ass, Peter Bell can endure no more and sobs aloud. After ten months' melancholy he becomes "a good and honest man."

"Peter Bell" is a very bold experiment, for one would expect such a serious subject as the regeneration of a sinful man to be treated with greater dignity. It is not surprising that the poem has seemed ridiculous to many. But, when Hazlitt visited Wordsworth at Alfoxden and heard the poet read "Peter Bell" aloud in the open air, "the comment made upon it by his face and voice was very different from that of some later critics! Whatever might be thought of the poem 'his face was as a book where men might read strange matters,' and he announced the fate of his hero in prophetic tones."[11] Over the years, Wordsworth subdued the humor and removed several passages of satire objectionable to respected friends. But he never tampered with the tributes to the courageous ass. Nor did he ever yield his conviction of the importance of Peter's discovery "That man's heart is a holy thing."

"Goody Blake and Harry Gill" and "Simon Lee"

"Goody Blake and Harry Gill" comes closest to the kind of poem Wordsworth told Wrangham might be written for circulation as a broadside ballad. The poet adapts the voice and idiom of a rustic commentator and projects his story in a strain of ballad homiletics at once "sophisticated and grotesque." He took the "true story" from Erasmus Darwin's *Zoönomia,* stated as happening in Warwickshire, and located it in Dorsetshire where he had come to know firsthand the acute suffering among impoverished peasants during the severe winter.

The poet quickly engages the sympathy of the reader for Goody Blake, a poor old dame who lives alone in an unsheltered cottage. Sometimes, when the frost is past enduring and her poor old bones ache from the cold, this *canty* dame leaves her meager fire to break sticks from the hedge of the lusty drover Harry Gill. The climax comes when, long suspecting her trespasses, Harry one frosty night watches to seize old Goody Blake. But he becomes the victim of his own folly; when he seizes and threatens her, she kneels and prays:

> She prayed, her withered hand uprearing,
> While Harry held her by the arm—
> "God! who art never out of hearing,
> O may he never more be warm!"
> The cold, cold moon above her head,
> Thus on her knees did Goody pray;
> Young Harry heard what she had said:
> And icy cold he turned away.

Harry piles on three riding coats and pins blankets about him, "Yet still his jaws and teeth they chatter." Never will Harry Gill be warm again.

In the fulfillment of the curse, the borderland between magic and psychology is bridged. Wordsworth stated in the 1800 Preface that in "Goody Blake and Harry Gill" he wished to draw attention "to the truth that the power of the human imagination is sufficient to produce such changes in our physical nature as might appear almost miraculous." Goody's curse is made the clear agent of justifiable vengeance. Though Goody Blake is caught stealing, the moral law supports her in inflicting upon Harry Gill perpetual cold. To bear home his moral, the poet closes with a wry twist of ballad piety: "Now think, ye farmers all, I pray/Of Goody Blake and Harry Gill!"

"Simon Lee, the Old Huntsman" is a poem about one of Wordsworth's neighbors near Alfoxden. In his youth Simon Lee had been a merry huntsman to the squires of Alfoxden; no one could outrun him or surpass him in the chase. But in old age he was bereft of health and he suffered neglect and poverty. He had become so enfeebled that one day, when the narrator was passing by, Simon was incapable of coping with the single root of an old tree. The poet, who proffered his help, easily severed the root with a single blow of the ax; and tears of thanks poured forth from the grateful old man. The incident of the root-cutting is told with matter-of-fact faithfulness, even a trace of humor; but the paradoxical moral is pronounced in prophetic tones:

> —I've heard of hearts unkind, kind deeds
> With coldness still returning;
> Alas! the gratitude of men
> Hath oftener left me mourning.

"Simon Lee" was often laughed at, chiefly because of the extreme rudeness of its style. The language is prosy and shockingly realistic: "His ancles they are swoln and thick;/His legs are thin and dry." Wordsworth's art is unpretentious, yet it is still effective. If we can reject the temptation to laugh or to be sentimental, we will find that the poet has prepared us carefully for the psychological paradox at the end.

Three "Complaints"

"The Mad Mother," "The Complaint of a Forsaken Indian Woman," and "The Last of the Flock" are "complaints." The complaint is a ballad form in a pattern already set by Percy and especially adapted to Wordsworth's purposes; for the story is told, as in a dramatic monologue, by the person most deeply concerned and the speaker's feelings are made a significant part of it. Each of these three ballads is set up in ten-line stanzas with the meter made "more lyrical and rapid" in order to engage the reader's sympathy. In one of the complaints, "The Mad Mother," Wordsworth drives deep into the piteous incoherence of her derangement, "in which from the increased sensibility the sufferer's attention is abruptly drawn off by every trifle, and at the same instant plucked back again by the one despotic thought" (as Coleridge admiringly put it). The circumstances, Wordsworth tells us, were based on a story told him by "a lady in Bristol" who had herself seen such a woman as he described.

"The Complaint of a Forsaken Indian Woman," taken from an account the poet had read in Hearne's *Journey from Hudson Bay,* was avowedly written to "follow the fluxes and refluxes of the mind . . . by accompanying the last struggles of a human being at the approach of death, cleaving in solitude to life and society." The eddying of thought and a very fine use of a double refrain create the artistic effect, but sentimentalism makes this tragic ballad less appealing to most readers than "The Mad Mother." The third of Wordsworth's complaints, "The Last of the Flock," based on an incident that occurred in the village of Holford, close by Alfoxden, is far more interesting than the other two complaints. It centers on the anguish of a shepherd who is forced in time of need to sell his precious flock in order to keep his children from starving to death. That he loves his children less as a consequence demonstrates the profound psychological effects of economic disaster.

Two Didactic Anecdotes

Two poems, "Anecdote for Fathers" and "We Are Seven," are both founded on fact and involve the questioning of children. In "Anecdote for Fathers" the child was a son of Wordsworth's friend Basil Montagu; and the boy had been two or three years under the poet's care. Dorothy found the boy a "perpetual

pleasure," but Wordsworth complained that "he lies like a little devil." The
full title on its first appearance read "Anecdote for Fathers, Shewing How the
Art of Lying May be Taught." In 1800, "the Art of Lying" was changed to
"the Practice of Lying" in the subtitle, and in 1845 the subtitle was dropped
for a Latin epigram from Eusebius which, translated, means: "Restrain your
eagerness, for I shall speak falsely if you force me."

In the poem, the reader overhears the extrarational wish of the child to be
in another place; when the boy is questioned by his father, and when he is
pushed still harder, his wish is bolstered by still another statement that is an
outright lie. Wordsworth wanted to show that a child's feelings have their
own inner laws; if an adult mind, with its logical ideas of cause and effect, intrudes itself into the intuitive mind of a child, distortions and untruths result.
Some persons consider Wordsworth's poem to be a conscious refutation of
Godwin's belief that lying is unnatural and merely the product of an evil social system. The poet learned quite a different lesson from his "dearest boy."

"We are Seven" is founded on a conversation the poet had with a little
girl at Goodrich Castle in 1793. Wordsworth composed the last stanza first,
having begun with the last line; when he needed an opening stanza to complete it, Coleridge supplied it impromptu. Wordsworth's aim in writing this
poem was to show "the obscurity and perplexity which in childhood attend
our notion of death, or rather our utter inability to admit that notion." He
acknowledged in his comments on the "Ode on Immortality" that nothing
was more difficult for him in childhood than to admit the notion of death as
a state applicable to his own being. In "We Are Seven" Wordsworth states
that the little girl cannot accept the idea of death because of feelings of animal vivacity:

> —A simple Child,
> That lightly draws its breath,
> And feels its life in every limb,
> What should it know of death?

This feeling is different from "a sense of the indomitableness of the spirit
within me," which the poet says possessed him in childhood. In either case,
however, the strong sense of personal identity and the consequent impossi-
bility on the part of the child of accepting the idea of personal annihilation
are the same.

Because of the cumbrous intermixture of the humorous with the exquisite and the sublime in "We Are Seven," the poem quickly became a favorite
with the parodists. One of the choicest parodies is Max Beerbohm's carica-

ture of Wordsworth holding an umbrella while cross-questioning a sad-looking urchin in the rain. But Wordsworth's poem was also very popular. There were many single copies printed surreptitiously and circulated in the way broadside ballads were. In the Lilly Library at Indiana University there is a copy of the ballad printed on a single sheet in seven different languages, one of them Japanese.

Four Nature Poems

Among the experimental ballads there are four nature poems that epitomize Wordsworth's faith—"To My Sister," "Lines Written in Early Spring," "Expostulation and Reply," and "The Tables Turned." They are set forth in language which is neither that of a native nor of a child but that of a speaker created by the poet. Coleridge in *Biographia Literaria* deplored Wordsworth's undue predilection for the *dramatic* form in certain of the ballads; but in these poems, except for the opening query by Matthew in "Expostulation and Reply," the poet is everywhere speaking through a persona. Moreover, the language he uses bears a close relationship to the genius of English language at its simple best.

"To My Sister," the first of these poems to be written, celebrates with a "fine, careless rapture" the coming of spring warmth. One early March day at Alfoxden, the speaker felt overpoweringly the joy of spring—"Each minute sweeter than before"—and sent word to his sister to put on quickly her woodland dress and come forth to spend the day with him in idleness. They need no book, he urges, for "It is the hour of feeling."

> One moment now may give us more
> Than years of toiling reason:
> Our minds shall drink at every pore
> The spirit of the season.

The ethic Wordsworth is expressing is that joy, serenity, and love itself would inevitably flow into and forth from the human heart if only it would surrender itself to the vital, joyous spirit everywhere found in nature.

The poem "Expostulation and Reply" and its companion, "The Tables Turned," were the result "of a conversation with a friend who was somewhat unreasonably attached to books of moral philosophy." The friend was William Hazlitt, who visited Wordsworth at Alfoxden at the end of May. Wordsworth felt that the book learning to which the young Hazlitt was addicted, especially the cold intellectualism of Godwin, would lead men into an arid desert of mechanical rationalism. He felt that true knowledge must be founded upon experience freshly received through the senses.

Thus in "Expostulation and Reply," when Wordsworth's friend (the Matthew of the poem) reproaches the poet for sitting idle half a day on his "old grey stone" and for neglecting his book learning, Wordsworth spiritedly made reply:

> The eye—it cannot choose but see;
> We cannot bid the ear be still;
> Our bodies feel, where'er they be,
> Against or with our will.
>
> Nor less I deem that there are Powers
> Which of themselves our minds impress;
> That we can feed this mind of ours
> In a wise passiveness.
>
> Think you, 'mid all this mighty sum
> Of things for ever speaking,
> That nothing of itself will come,
> But we must still be seeking?

What Wordsworth is saying is that the senses furnish men with the primary data out of which they build this moral and spiritual life, and that there are "Powers" in nature that will help in this process if we are calm and receptive.

In "The Tables Turned" the poet, with a light touch of extravagance, calls upon his friend to leave the "dull and endless strife" with books:

> Come forth into the light of things,
> Let Nature be your Teacher.
>
> She has a world of ready wealth,
> Our minds and hearts to bless—
> Spontaneous wisdom breathed by health,
> Truth breathed by cheerfulness.
>
> One impulse from a vernal wood
> May teach you more of man,
> Of moral evil and of good,
> Than all the sages can.

No one should seriously suppose that Wordsworth was here or elsewhere declaring himself an enemy of book learning. He obviously did not mean that a person was to give up reading any more than that *he* was to sit in permanent passiveness on an old gray stone. He was protesting against the overbearing encroachment of the "meddling intellect."

In "Lines Written in Early Spring" a sad thought intrudes itself. On a mid-April day, when the poet reclines beside the brook that runs through the grounds at Alfoxden, he feels his human soul linked with pleasure to nature's fair works. Yet in the midst of a world that seems to be meant to be free and joyous, and that appears to be so among the flowers, the birds, and the budding twigs, man alone is joyless. France at that time had ruthlessly invaded Switzerland; and the speaker, though surrounded by joyousness, was grieved, had "reason to lament/What man has made of man."

These four nature poems not only express the profundities of Wordsworth's faith; they sing with a rhythmic gaiety. The style is markedly simple; yet the simplicity is given everlasting appeal by means of lilting rhythms and repetitions. For example, the last line of each poem (except "The Tables Turned") serves as a refrain. All have verbal surprises, such as "wise passiveness," "spontaneous wisdom"; aphorisms, "we murder to dissect"; and bare precept, "Come forth into the light of things." The most notable stylistic feature is a playful exaggeration, which has frequently been misunderstood. But it need not and should not be: when shorn of its stylistic exaggeration, the poet's basic teaching easily reveals itself. His precepts spring from the very roots of his experience and are so universally true that they still speak through these poems to the condition of many human spirits.

"Lines Composed a Few Miles above Tintern Abbey"

Wordsworth and his sister left Alfoxden on 25 June 1798, and, after a week with Coleridge in Stowey, they journeyed to Bristol where Cottle was preparing *Lyrical Ballads* for the press. After a week spent working with him, William felt a longing to see once more the valleys and hills of Wales, through which he had wandered five years before. He wanted to share with Dorothy the beauteous scenes which, despite a long absence, he had never forgotten. So he took her on a four-day ramble along the Wye River, during which they visited the beautiful ruins of Tintern Abbey and proceeded as far north as Goodrich Castle before returning the way they had come from Bristol.

At one point in their wanderings up the river from Tintern Abbey, William led Dorothy to a vantage point that opened to their view a magnificent prospect. There in the tranquillity of a sycamore's shade the poet's mind traveled back past that day of ecstasy five years earlier to the still further-removed time of carefree schooldays and forward again through fleeting shadows to the present. To one "so long a worshipper of Nature," a multitude of memories crowded to a climax of joy in the present stillness of his mind, and a poem was born. Wordsworth afterward related that he began composing it upon leaving Tintern after crossing the Wye, and that he concluded it just as he was entering Bristol. Not a line of it was altered and not any part of it written down until he had reached the city. The full title of this now famous poem is "Lines Composed a Few Miles above Tintern Abbey, on Revisiting the Banks of the Wye during a Tour, July 13, 1798." The title is not factually accurate, for, as Wordsworth says, the poem was composed after leaving Tintern Abbey. But the prospect described is the one as seen a few miles above the abbey.

The travelers seem to have taken William Gilpin's *Tour of the Wye* with them. In the opening stanza of "Tintern Abbey," at any rate, the landscape prospect seen from "under this dark sycamore" is described overtly in picturesque terms and the closing lines appear to owe a debt to Gilpin and there are many echoes of other writers as well[12]:

> Five years have past; five summers, with the length
> Of five long winters! and again I hear
> These waters, rolling from their mountain-springs
> With a soft inland murmur.—Once again
> Do I behold these steep and lofty cliffs,
> That on a wild secluded scene impress
> Thoughts of more deep seclusion; and connect
> The landscape with the quiet of the sky.
> The day is come when I again repose
> Here, under this dark sycamore, and view
> These plots of cottage-ground, these orchard-tufts,
> Which at this season, with their unripe fruits,
> Are clad in one green hue, and lose themselves
> 'Mid groves and copses. Once again I see
> These hedge-rows, hardly hedge-rows, little lines
> Of sportive wood run wild: these pastoral farms,
> Green to the very door; and wreaths of smoke
> Sent up, in silence, from among the trees!
> With some uncertain notice, as might seem

Of vagrant dwellers in the houseless woods,
Or of some Hermit's cave, where by his fire
The Hermit sits alone.

There is no lack of significant pictorial detail in this opening passage. The landscape is described with more than usual care, and its many images are rendered with great clearness for the eye and the mind to rest upon. Yet there is also much that points to an inward, psychical response. The waters of the river are heard "rolling from their mountain springs," but the full impression is not of a river seen or heard but of one felt in its continuing entity as it winds from its mountain home to its confrontation "inland" by the tides of the sea. Wordsworth has moved from the river of the outer physical world to a river whose existence is an inner prospect of the mind.

So, too, the "steep and lofty cliffs" before him "on a wild secluded scene" impress "*thoughts of more deep seclusion.*" Additional features of the landscape show man and nature as mixing together, and their combining becomes significant inwardly and symbolically. The grass of the pastoral farms is "green to the very doors"; plots of cottage ground "lose themselves in groves and copses"; hedgerows and woodlands intermingle; wreaths of smoke (man-created) lose themselves among the houseless woods where men dwell. Then, somehow, the upward movement of the lofty cliffs and smoke connect the living, inhabited landscape with the quiet of the sky in an ascent that suggests a spiritual union of the whole. Wordsworth has rendered a masterful landscape in these verses, selecting and dramatizing its pictorial features; but he has also endowed it with inward symbolic significance. In his landscape of the Wye, man, nature, and the divine world are interfused—all exist in a mighty unity.

The landscape before him starts the ruminative process, and he thinks of all that the memory of this beautiful scene has meant to him during his five years' absence. He believes that he owes to these beauteous forms three blessings: first, sensations sweet, physical, and restorative, "felt in the blood," which pass even into his inmost mind with quieting effect; second, feelings unperceived and unremembered but which mysteriously guide him in the performance of kind and unselfish acts, such as the severing of the tree root for old Simon Lee; third, and crowning all, he was lifted at intervals to a mystic vision whence he was enabled to "see into the life of things." It is unlikely that Wordsworth experienced this last and highest gift until perhaps a year or so before his second visit to the Wye. But restorative sensations nourished his physical and moral being often over the years.

As he looks upon the "steep woods and lofty cliffs," he recalls the image of himself as he came that way five years before. He sees himself as one who then sought refuge from tormenting mental conflict by flinging himself into physical delight in nature like one driven by insatiable thirst. But now "That time is past/And all its aching joys are now no more/And all its dizzy raptures." The loss, however, is compensated by "other gifts" more precious. The sounding cataracts that haunted him on his first visit and the din and turmoil in the cities that followed it have been replaced by the "soft, inland murmur" of the river and by the silent beauty of the landscape. The new-found tranquillity before him induces a quieting response within. He now has a gentler outlook on the tragedy of humanity ("Nor harsh nor grating, though of ample power/To chasten and subdue"). And he gains a sense of presence deeply interfused around him and in him, illimitable and united in one joyous harmony of all existence:

> And I have felt
> A presence that disturbs me with the joy
> Of elevated thoughts; a sense sublime
> Of something far more deeply interfused,
> Whose dwelling is the light of setting suns,
> And the round ocean and the living air,
> And the blue sky, and in the mind of man:
> A motion and a spirit, that impels
> All thinking things, all objects of all thought,
> And rolls through all things.

Wordsworth's return to the Wye in 1798 supplied him with a montage (the superimposition of one experience upon another) that confirmed his belief in the unity of past and present, as well as his belief in the unity of man and nature. The chief human agency in the reconciling work was Dorothy, who was in the precise stage of development that the poet had been five years before. To Dorothy still belonged the ecstatic, primitive delight in natural things that Wordsworth recognizes can no longer be his. He does not "murmur" at his own change but projects his own present into his sister's future in a warmly felt and generous prayer for her as a worshiper of nature. Nature in its beauty is a source of joy and of healing thoughts that will minister to Dorothy in her future need as it has ministered to the poet in the past. Wordsworth's faith in nature's power to bring comfort to his sister was a complex, intuitive belief comprised of memory, sensation, feeling, knowledge and half-knowledge, moral awareness, and mystical insight—all united in the powerful solvent of his mind.

"Tintern Abbey" was added to *Lyrical Ballads,* then being readied for the press, and became the concluding poem in the book. It was not one of the experimental poems; indeed, it has nothing to do with them except that its language, like those of other personal poems in the volume, keeps to the high road of poetic tradition established by Shakespeare, Spenser, and Milton. Its music is impassioned, which in Wordsworth's view made it comparable to an ode. Its repetitive words, phrases, and patterns give to the flowing rhythms a wonderfully resonant and noble beauty. The poetic expression of the impact of the scenic landscape upon the innermost recesses of the poet's mind was as spontaneous as it was powerful. The poem took shape while his feelings were overflowing with joy and while his faith in the power of nature to dispel "fear or pain or grief" was still at high tide. In after years he qualified and subdued the beliefs articulated in "Tintern Abbey." But he never lost delight in the simple converse of nature or his faith that all created things can bring pleasure to the sensitive person impelled by love.

The Publication and Reception of *Lyrical Ballads*

Lyrical Ballads appeared anonymously in mid-September 1798, without a hint to reveal the presence of more than one author. Wordsworth and Coleridge craved anonymity in their venture; to ensure it, they had at the last moment removed Coleridge's "Lewti," a lyric that had appeared in print in the *Morning Post* and was known to be his work; and they substituted for it "The Nightingale." The secret of authorship was so well kept that neither the authors' names nor even the fact of dual authorship became generally known until announced in the preface to the second edition.

Curiously enough, after Cottle had run off a few copies of *Lyrical Ballads* under his own imprint, he sold the edition to J. and A. Arch, a London bookseller, probably because he had become alarmed by Robert Southey, who warned Cottle that the work would not sell. Southey, who was still estranged from Coleridge, gave the new book a rough handling when he reviewed it. Not a month had passed following publication before Southey's review appeared in the *Critical Review* of October 1798. Southey, who claimed his understanding of the story of "The Ancient Mariner" was insufficient to analyze it, dubbed it "a Dutch attempt at German sublimity." He also condemned "The Idiot Boy": "No tale less deserved the labour that appears to have been bestowed upon this." He thought the serious pieces to be the better part of the volume, for example, "The Female Vagrant," but he considered the experiment a failure "because it has been tried upon uninteresting subjects."

All the reviewers followed Southey's lead in finding fault with "The Ancient Mariner." Dr. Burney in the *Monthly Review* of June 1799 thought "The Rime of the Ancient Mariner" "the strangest story of a cock and bull that we ever saw on paper." He said the experiments were unworthy as poetry, but he admired touches of genius and wished "to see another volume by the same hand, written on more elevated subjects and in a more cheerful disposition." The only review in full and intelligent sympathy with the novel "experiment" was written by Francis Wrangham, a friend of Wordsworth; it appeared in the *British Critic* of October 1799. Wrangham thought that the intermediate part of "The Ancient Mariner" was too long and that the antiquated words might better have been omitted entirely. But the poems of the rest of the volume, he wrote, have high merit and some of them "a very high rank of merit."

Mrs. Coleridge wrote to her husband in Germany (where he and the Wordsworths were traveling when the volume was finally published) that the *Lyrical Ballads* were "laughed at and disliked by all with very few excepted," but her blunt appraisal does not coincide entirely with the facts. The volume eventually sold much better than the authors themselves had expected, and it was liked by a much greater number of people. Four editions (added to in the meantime) were called for by 1805. As proved in the long run, the instinctive responses of young William Hazlitt, though not those of a reviewer, were prophetic of the final evaluation to be placed on the new poems. On Hazlitt's visit to Alfoxden during the last days of May 1798, he had free access to Wordsworth's contributions to *Lyrical Ballads* then still in manuscript. Hazlitt later recorded his impressions in "My First Acquaintance with Poets":

I dipped into a few of these with great satisfaction, and with the faith of a novice. . . . I was not critically or sceptically inclined. I saw touches of truth and nature, and took the rest for granted. But in "The Thorn," "The Mad Mother," and "The Complaint of a [Forsaken] Indian Woman," I felt that deeper power and pathos which has since been acknowledged . . . as the characteristics of this author; and the sense of a new style and a new spirit in poetry came over me. It had to me something of the effect that arises from the turning up of the fresh soil, or of the first welcome breath of Spring.

Chapter Three
Lyrical Ballads, 1800

On 15 September 1798 William, Dorothy, and Coleridge sailed from Yarmouth to Hamburg, Germany. They saw the sights and visited with Klopstock, the German poet, but separated at the beginning of October. Coleridge left for Ratzeburg, and the Wordsworths, for no discoverable reason, settled at Goslar, at the edge of the Harz Mountains, to spend the winter. It turned out to be one of the coldest winters on record. As a consequence, the poet and his sister found themselves isolated in a foreign country, with no books except the few they had brought with them, no social amenities, and little opportunity to learn the German language, the chief purpose for which they had come.

Isolated in Goslar, the Wordsworths were thrown back upon themselves and upon thoughts of their homeland. To the poet in that alien environment fervent recollections of his childhood and other memories came with an intensity he had never before known. Exile fed the springs of inspiration; again he was possessed by the "creative breeze," and it was blowing now, not gently, but as "A tempest, a redundant energy." The result was some of Wordsworth's finest poetry, differing sharply from the Alfoxden poems, which were based for the most part upon everyday events that had transpired shortly before they were written.

Reminiscence or recollection had already appeared in "Tintern Abbey," but in the Goslar poems it was raised and intensified to the highest degree. Within the recesses of his own mind Wordsworth recovered those "spots of time"—moments that returned to consciousness out of the depths of the past—leaping "from hiding places ten years deep." A most notable list of poems composed during the frigid winter at Goslar attests to the rich new sources of inspiration released in the poet. These poems include the matchless pictures of his boyhood that later were to become part of *The Prelude,* the Lucy poems, "Lucy Gray," "The Poet's Epitaph," the Matthew poems, and "Ruth."

The Lucy Poems

The five elegiac pieces known as the Lucy poems are all associated with the stay in Germany, though one of them seems not to have been written until April 1801. Four are in ballad stanza and reveal Wordsworth's interest in this form, quickened by his purchase at Hamburg of a copy of Percy's *Reliques*. In those lonely months in Germany the love of England was firmly reestablished. In that nostalgic yearning and an aching memory of sufficiency now lost, the Lucy poems had their origin. Robert Frost once said that poetry often begins in lovesickness or in homesickness. The Lucy poems seem to have begun in both:

> I travelled among unknown men,
>   In lands beyond the sea;
> Nor, England! did I know till then
>   What love I bore to thee.
>
> 'Tis past, that melancholy dream!
>   Nor will I quit thy shore
> A second time; for still I seem
>   To love thee more and more.
>
> Among thy mountains did I feel
>   The joy of my desire;
> And she I cherished turned her wheel
>   Beside an English fire.
>
> Thy mornings showed, thy nights concealed
>   The bowers where Lucy played;
> And thine too is the last green field
>   That Lucy's eyes surveyed.[1]

The Lucy whose loss the poet mourns is a person; but one does not know who she was—nor, indeed, if there ever was a Lucy. It is possible, of course, to deny any particular identity to Lucy and to hypothesize that she was a purely ideal creation existing solely in the imagination of the poet. The name of Lucy had become a sort of commonplace in elegiac poetry. It occurs in Percy's *Reliques* in a poem, "Lucy and Colin," written by Thomas Tichell and elsewhere in poems by George Lyttleton, Edward Moore, Thomas Chatterton, William Collins, and Samuel Rogers; Wordsworth was acquainted with most of them. It would be rash, however, knowing Wordsworth's strong tendency toward the autobiographical, to say that Lucy is entirely fictitious.

A number of candidates have been offered as her living counterpart: Annette Vallon, who is finally rejected by means of the poems themselves (that Lucy was English and a child of nature disposes of any possible connection with Annette); Mary Hutchinson, his future wife toward whom his heart was now returning (why, then, should she be dead?); Margaret Hutchinson, her sister, whom perhaps in early youth the poet had loved and who, indeed, had died of consumption in 1796; Mary of Esthwaite, perhaps a real but unknown love of Wordsworth's schoolboy days; and his sister Dorothy, for whom the strongest case can be made.

There is definite evidence that the name "Lucy" is connected with Dorothy. In a letter to Coleridge of 1802, Lucy is identified by Wordsworth as Dorothy in the Glow-Worm poem ("Among all lovely things"). Coleridge, who thought Dorothy was Lucy, sent Thomas Poole a copy of "A Slumber did my Spirit seal" and added by way of explanation that "Most probably in some gloomier moment [the poet] had fancied the moment when his sister might die." F. W. Bateson explained the death and sexlessness of these love poems by conjecturing that Wordsworth was falling in love with Dorothy and that he subconsciously dealt with the dangerous and explosive situation by symbolically killing her. But the sensational incest wish and the psychic burial theory have not found acceptance.

Lucy may have had her origin in some real person or persons, but in the poems she has been sublimated into something much more than a person. She is an ideal figure of English maidenhood to which all the poet's feelings about love, women, and nature are attached. She is seen entirely from within the poet; at times, she seems barely human, ready to lapse back into nature. Lucy is "a *thing* that could not feel/The touch of earthly years." There is no real difference between her living and dying, except in the consciousness of the survivor. The unresolved ingredient of the poet's thought is the agonizing search for steadfastness and permanence behind nature as idealized in the person of Lucy. His consciousness is overwhelmed by the fateful passing of youth, beauty, and love. "But she is in her grave, and, oh,/The difference to me!"

The first poem in the "Lucy" cycle, "Strange fits of passion," is constructed around Lucy's cottage. The poet pictures himself one moonlit evening as riding on horseback toward her house. Mary Moorman reconstructs the setting as true to Racedown and the entire poem as a personal memory of a true event in the lives of William and Dorothy. Of greater interest than the identity of Lucy, however, is the mental condition of the speaker. "In one of those sweet dreams I slept,/Kind Nature's gentlest boon," he says of his ride to Lucy's cottage. His person is in a hypnotic state, a creative sleep of the senses when the "soul" and imagination are most alive, kept in focus by the moon and reinforced by the rhythmic repetition of the horse's hoof beats. Then, when he rides uphill and the moon suddenly "sets" behind the cottage, the hypnotic mood is broken and he associates the "setting" with her death:

> What fond and wayward thoughts will slide
> Into a Lover's head!
> "O mercy!" to myself I cried,
> "If Lucy should be dead!"

In the Lucy poems, Wordsworth effectively employs metaphors and symbols—and in none more so than in the celebrated "She dwelt among the untrodden ways." This lyric in its first version as sent to Coleridge consisted of five stanzas. It was cut to three for publication in 1800 and certainly lost nothing thereby. The middle stanza contains the famous metaphors:

> A violet by a mossy stone
> Half hidden from the eye!
> —Fair as a star, when only one
> Is shining in the sky.

These metaphors and the first stanza illuminate each other. The isolation of the violet and the star set off their beauty and the comparison to Lucy; they, in turn, enhance her beauty. Also the violet and the star seem humanized by being compared to Lucy, but at the same time the comparison of Lucy to the lovely but inanimate objects in nature keeps her from being warmly human. Lucy is far removed, for example, from Keats's fair love with ripening breast in his "Bright Star" sonnet.

The Lucy elegies are also a triumph of understatement; especially is this characteristic in "She dwelt among the untrodden ways." Here understatement achieves its full effect in the last four words: "But she is in her grave, and, oh,/The difference to me!" Among the Romantic poets, only Walter Savage Landor could use restraint with anything like Wordsworth's dynamism, as in "Rose Alymer,"—"A night of memories and of sighs/I consecrate to thee." But a comparison of these two justly famed elegiac conclusions reveals at once that Wordsworth's has the greater power.

"Three years she grew in sun and shower" was written in the spring of 1799 after Wordsworth and his sister had left Goslar and were walking through the Harz forest to Nordhausen. A poem of seven six-line stanzas, it is the only one of the Lucy poems not in ballad meter. In six of the stanzas Nature undertakes to oversee Lucy's growth in her daily comradeship with the vital impulses of beauty and delight that everywhere surround her, for she is "Nature's child." Nowhere has the poet more simply and delicately described the twofold power of Nature to quicken and to calm than in her words about Lucy:

> Myself will to my darling be
> Both law and impulse: and with me
> The Girl, in rock and plain,
> In earth and heaven, in glade and bower,
> Shall feel an overseeing power
> To kindle or restrain.

As Wordsworth describes the ministry of natural beauty in molding the loveliness of Lucy, the verse reaches a lyrical perfection scarcely equaled elsewhere by the poet:

> The floating clouds their state shall lend
> To her; for her the willow bend;
> Nor shall she fail to see
> Even in the motions of the Storm
> Grace that shall mould the Maiden's form
> By silent sympathy.

> The stars of midnight shall be dear
> To her; and she shall lean her ear
> In many a secret place
> Where rivulets dance their wayward round
> And beauty born of murmuring sound
> Shall pass into her face.

The poet's representation in this lyric of the molding discipline that Nature brings to Lucy merges with the more personal image he has given elsewhere of Dorothy responding to Nature's influence.

"A slumber did my spirit seal"—the "sublime epitaph," as Coleridge called it—consists of but two four-line stanzas. But in these eight lines Wordsworth achieves a masterful compression of poetic power. In the cryptic first line, which summarizes the thought of the first stanza, the poet pictures himself in a hypnotic mystic sleep. His being is in sublime repose, as it was in the opening lyric of the cycle when he was approaching Lucy's cottage—"In one of those sweet dreams I slept." He is confidently self-possessed in his thoughts about his loved one; he cannot imagine Lucy's death. Then suddenly she is gone:

> No motion has she now, no force;
> She neither hears nor sees;
> Rolled round in earth's diurnal course,
> With rocks and stones and trees.

Irony, not often used by Wordsworth, pervades the first stanza of this elegy. The slumber that captivated him, but that he could not associate with Lucy—"She seemed a thing that could not feel/The touch of earthly years"—is suddenly hers forever as she sleeps the sleep of death. She, who once seemed so alive that her lover was lulled into the false security of thinking she could never be without life, is now absolutely and irrevocably without motion, vitality, or feeling. She, who seemed to exist so that the passing of time meant nothing, has now become an inseparable part of the imperative cosmic forces of consuming time.

Something unique has gone from his life, but there is no thought of immortality. He has been living under the assumption—supported by mystic moments of insight when slumber sealed his spirit[2]—that there is steadfastness, serenity, and permanent power behind Nature. In "Three years she grew," Nature spoke and declared her dual force: "Myself will to my darling be/Both *law* and *impulse*." Law, especially natural law, is permanent and steady; but impulse, the poet learns, is uncertain and wayward. He had been deluded by the thought of Lucy's deathlessness. When at last she is in the grave, he finds himself time's fool. For Lucy had become so completely the sublimation of existence that, with her passing, he is overwhelmed by an awareness never before realized of the mutability of all existence.

The Lucy poems are sublimated love poems of sustained pathos. They are unexcelled in the use of simple language to express pure and spontaneous emotion. In addition, their symbolic import places them among the most perfect expressions of Wordsworth's sense of mutability. By them, we are made sublimely aware of the tragic realities of our frail human existence.

"Lucy Gray; or, Solitude," "Ruth," and "Poor Susan"

"Lucy Gray; or, Solitude," a haunting ballad of childhood, is founded upon a true story remembered by Dorothy of a little girl lost in a snowstorm. The suggestion has been made that "Lucy Gray" should be placed in the Lucy cycle; indeed, it has been conjectured that this ballad is the starting point of all the Lucy poems. The first three and the last two stanzas do make a complete Lucy poem; also, like others in the series, it was written at Goslar in ballad meter.

Lucy Gray is a solitary child and belongs to the world of wild and innocent animals—the fawn, the hare, and the roe. She is associated with all that is free and lovely in the natural world; moreover, she is "The sweetest thing that ever grew/Beside a human door." One day her father, fearing a stormy night, calls upon Lucy to go to the town with a lantern to light the way for her mother through the snow. The child goes willingly, blithe as "the mountain roe"; but, when the storm "came on before its time," Lucy lost her way. The wretched parents, who search all that night, find no trace of their little girl. Next morning they discover the child's footmarks and trace them to the middle of the wooden plank over a stream—"And further there were none!"

In his note to "Lucy Gray" Wordsworth expresses a hope that "The way in which the incident was treated and the spiritualizing of the character might furnish hints for contrasting the imaginative influences which I have endeavoured to throw over common life with Crabbe's matter of fact style of treating subjects of the same kind." In Wordsworth's ballad Lucy dies, but no corpse is found. Perhaps, the poet suggests, the child did not die in any natural sense; she may have been translated into an identification with immortal Nature. Though Lucy Gray is specially vulnerable to death, she is also specially impervious to it. In lonesome places the "living child" may still be seen as she trips along, or she may be heard singing "a solitary song/That whistles in the wind."

"Ruth" was written at Goslar from memories of a story Wordsworth had of a wanderer in Somersetshire. The verse form is a six-line stanza resembling that of Drayton's "Dowsabel," which was in the copy of Percy's *Reliques* that Wordsworth had purchased in Hamburg. The subject of woman's unhappy love frequently appears in the *Reliques,* two cases of which exactly parallel that of "Ruth."

"Ruth" is a tale of courtship and desertion, in which Wordsworth shows a further range of his awareness; he extends particularly the boundaries of his thought about nature's teachings. Ruth was not seven years old when her father remarried; and the child, slighted by her stepmother, became a solitary wanderer over the countryside. When grown to lovely womanhood, she was courted by a young soldier just returned from the war in America. A handsome youth, he enthralled Ruth with his stories of life among the Indians and of their idyllic existence. Ruth readily accepted his proposal to make her home with him in the wild woods of America; and they were wed.

The youth had grown up in the eye of nature, but in a wild land he had been exposed to unsettling sights and sounds. From unworthy men he absorbed evil ways and himself became "the slave of low desires." The love of Ruth had at first stirred in him higher and better thoughts, but these soon left him. He deserted her to return to his life "with roving bands of Indians in the West." Ruth, crazed by his betrayal and having no place to go, becomes a vagrant. She lives in the open and begs for her food by the roadside. Left to loneliness and neglect, the best she can hope for is the relief from "the engines of her pain" that madness brings her. The last she can expect is that her body shall lie buried "in the hallowed mould."

"Ruth" shows that in 1799 Wordsworth is not exuberantly proclaiming that all persons exposed to outdoor life will inevitably become morally upright. "Wild and voluptuous nature" can have a corrupting effect, as it did upon the fair youth from Georgia. And nature can be indifferent and cruel to a helpless human being, as it was to Ruth, who had "sore aches" and "body wretchedness,/From damp, and rain, and cold." Nature was not only the influence that shaped Ruth's beauty but "the tool that shaped her sorrow." Wordsworth had no illusion that city dwellers would be better off if they abandoned themselves to the raw wildness of country life.

Nor is personal responsibility in moral matters to be overlooked. The stepmother of Ruth by her cruel neglect is exposed as wholly culpable. Also the deserting husband is held up for severe condemnation. In the desertion theme, the poet may again have been expressing remorse for his treatment of Annette. In any event, Wordsworth reveals a perceptive understanding of Ruth's faithless husband—how he came to be the unstable person he was and why he acted the way he did. He also shows poignant pity for the abandoned Ruth. "Ruth" made severe demands upon Wordsworth's art and is of unequal quality. But he achieved in this narrative some noteworthy features already discussed, to which should be added the effective painting of the exotic splendors of North America (lines 49–84) taken from *Bartram's Travels* (1791).

"The Reverie of Poor Susan" Wordsworth himself dated in 1836 as having been written in 1797, but he later altered the date to "1801 or 1802" (a mistake, as the poem was published in 1800). Mary Moorman wonders if he did not write the poem in Germany in 1799, for the title is an exact translation of Bürger's "Das Arme Süsschen's Traum," his favorite in the volume of Bürger's poems that he had purchased at Hamburg. In February 1800, he wrote to Coleridge that he had found pleasure in reading Bürger, but he also complained of a lack of "distinct forms" and "feelings" in the German poet. "Poor Susan" is almost an answer to this defect in Bürger.

Susan turns from the wearisome dullness of city life to behold, through the window of imagination opened by the song of the caged thrush, the distinct forms and images of her country home from which she has been so long separated: "A mountain ascending, a vision of trees." As she looks upon the beauteous scene before her she is restored as if by miracle, and "her heart is in heaven." But, as quickly as the vision came, it faded away. Wordsworth isolates the feeling, yet in no way sentimentalizes Susan or her situation.

The Matthew Poems and "A Poet's Epitaph"

Among the memories of his youth that flowed with delicacy and clarity into Wordsworth's brooding mind at Goslar were those of his schooldays at Hawkshead. These memories were lovingly recorded in the Matthew poems in which the poet establishes contrasts between youth and age that center in the schoolboy and his schoolmaster, respectively. However, the Matthew of the poems is not a factual representation of Wordsworth's teacher, William Taylor, who dies in his thirty-third year. Rather, he is a composite and idealized figure having more affinities with an old traveling packman, who became attracted to the schoolboy and was his companion in many a ramble through the hills. The characteristics of this packman are set forth with some fullness in an unpublished manuscript now called "The Pedlar."[3] He had a serene and cheerful disposition and a stock of "home-felt" wisdom that he imparted to his young companion in whimsical stories and comments.

All the poems of the Matthew series, including elegies left in manuscript by Wordsworth, stress the old man's paradoxical temperament. The poem "Matthew" characteristically sets forth the wondrous incongruity of his sighs and tears:

> The sighs which Matthew heaved were sighs
> Of one tired out with fun and madness;
> The tears which came to Matthew's eyes
> Were tears of light, the dew of gladness.

In "Two April Mornings," Matthew is "As blithe a man as you could see/On a spring holiday," yet he utters "so sad a sigh" that it arouses his youthful companion with whom he is out walking to question him as to its cause. He replies that the resplendent April morning that gladdens them brings fresh into his mind a day just like it thirty years before. On that day he had come by chance to stand beside his nine-year-old daughter's grave, and he was filled with a poignant yearning for her:

> Six feet in earth my Emma lay;
> And yet, I loved her more,
> For so it seemed, than till that day
> I e'er had loved before.

When he turned to leave his daughter's grave, he met beside the churchyard yew "A blooming Girl, whose hair was wet/With points of morning dew." She was a vision of loveliness, a Lucy as it were come to life:

> A basket on her head she bare;
> Her brow was smooth and white:
> To see a child so very fair,
> It was a pure delight!
>
> No fountain from its rocky cave
> E'er tripped with foot so free;
> She seemed as happy as a wave
> That dances on the sea.

The fresh beauty of the living girl vividly recalled the fact of his daughter's sweet loveliness. But there are things the heart cannot replace. Matthew looked at the girl before him and looked again, and he was so pierced with longing or was so deterred by pain he could not wish her to be his. One of the strange facts of parental love is that a child of one's own cannot be replaced by one who is not. Years later the poet remembers this surprising ending to his old teacher's story, and in a final stanza he creates, in effect, a third April morning:

> Matthew is in his grave, yet now,
> Methinks, I see him stand,
> As at that moment, with a bough
> Of wilding in his hand.

In "The Fountain," the poet and his old teacher Matthew are seated together one beautiful morning beneath a spreading oak beside which a fountain gurgled. As they speak with open hearts, they release in friendship their inner thoughts. The fountain may be thought of as symbolizing in their dialogue the ebullient spirit of youth; the oak, the sober wisdom of age. The boy, responding to the joyous sound of the running water, calls upon the old man to sing some border song or witty rhyme that suits a summer mood. But Matthew at first disappoints the expectations of the boy. The old man looks at the fountain and observes how thoughtlessly and changelessly it flows. As a youthful, vigorous man, he often joyously lay beside this spring, but, now in old age, he is saddened by the losses he has suffered of "kindred laid in earth." He is compelled to feel a sorrow corresponding to the joy his human relationships once gave him. This is a "foolish strife," but it is indigenous to man and inevitable.

When the boy exclaims that he could be a son to him, the old man knows better: "Alas! that cannot be." Age retains so intense a memory of love, it takes away the power to form new attachments to replace those lost. But the sorrow must be borne; and Matthew, being a man of glee, in the end sings "About the crazy old church-clock,/And the bewildered chimes." Matthew has been "pressed by heavy laws," but he has not dried up. He has kept alive the mirth of youth to hide the sorrow of age. An energetic spirit still bubbles like a fountain within him and feeds the laughter that hides tears.

Matthew is a wondrously archetypal figure, particular and yet symbolic, a village schoolmaster and yet a kind of gnomic oracle. Paradoxes and opaque symbols subtly intertwine in the unfolding of his character. In "The Fountain," above the "witty rhymes" one hears the tolling paradox: "The wiser mind/Mourns less for what age takes away/Than what it leaves behind." And, at the close of "Two April Mornings," one sees Matthew "with a bough of wilding in his hand," symbol at once of gaiety and sorrow.

"A Poet's Epitaph," written in Goslar, is a satiric thrust at worldlings insensitive to a true poet's worth. Wordsworth addresses those who would approach his grave; and he cautions the politician, the lawyer, the divine, the scientist, and the moralist to give him wide berth. Men who devote themselves to rational analysis and unprofitable "getting and spending" are unworthy visitors. But the gallant soldier who lays aside his sword is welcome. And let the poet "with modest looks,/And clad in homely russet brown" come near. The picture of the poet is perhaps a self-portrait; at least it is a memorable one:

> He is retired as noontide dew,
> Or fountain in a noon-day grove;
> And you must love him, ere to you
> He will seem worthy of your love.

> The outward shows of sky and earth,
> Of hill and valley, he has viewed;
> And impulses of a deeper birth
> Have come to him in solitude.

Charles Lamb objected to "the vulgar satire upon parsons and lawyers in the beginning" and to the coarse use of an epithet, later removed, that intensified Wordsworth's attack upon the scientist by referring to his "pin-point of a soul." Lamb thought "All the rest is eminently good, and your own."

Pastorals: "The Brothers" and "Michael"

In early spring William and Dorothy left Goslar; and, after wandering about in Germany and briefly visiting Coleridge at Göttingen, they were back in England by May. And "right glad" they were, wrote William, "for we have learned to know its value." They headed northward to visit Mary Hutchinson at Sockburn-on-Tees, where her brother Tom had a farm. Coleridge, who joined them there, accompanied William on a walking tour of the Lakes, the chief object of which was to find a suitable place for him and his sister to live. In the exquisite valley of Grasmere William found the very cottage of Dorothy's dream and returned to Sockburn to fetch her. On a cold December day in 1799 they ended a wild winter journey at Dove Cottage, which became their home for the next eight years.

Grasmere was a peaceful spot, but did not force the poet to work in self-centered solitude. The brother and sister roamed the dales and hills alert with eager, questing eyes and hearts for the substance of poetry. Rural incidents such as Wordsworth had treated imaginatively in the first edition of *Lyrical Ballads* they found near at hand, but the narrative poems resulting from them differ in several important aspects from the narratives of his Alfoxden days. Two moving pastorals, "The Brothers" and "Michael," were written in the first year at Grasmere. Their focus, like that of the earlier poems, is on the psychology of passion; and the feeling developed in them gives importance to the action and situation, not the other way around. But in these pastorals there is no derangement caused by grief, as in "The Thorn" or "The Mad Mother." The passion has to do simply with the brave endurance of humble, rustic figures. And the passion is communicated not by "lyrical and rapid metre" nor in repetitious, excited utterance, as in "The Thorn," but in muted understatement. Gone, too, is the uncouth, colloquial language; in its place is a somewhat heightened, yet natural and easy, conversational tone that represented for Wordsworth a compromise between dramatic and poetic propriety.

"The Brothers" and "Michael" both have to do with man's attachment to place. At the time Wordsworth came to live at Dove Cottage, there was a decline in small properties in the Lake District. The factory system was driving the hand loom from the cottages, the loss of which spelled ruin for the proprietors. To Wordsworth, who thought that a small property was the principal support to the affections, such a loss was tragic. In a letter to Charles James Fox, the Whig politician possessing the greatest "sensibility of heart," Wordsworth explained that the tract of land possessed by the independent proprietors in the Lake Country "serves as a kind of permanent rallying point for their domestic feelings." A small farm is, as it were, a tablet upon which is recorded the history of a man's emotional life. Its permanent objects—its trees, its stone walls, its brooks—are bound up with memories of the past, associated with acts of kindness as in the rescue of a sheep or acts of love involving one's child.

Thus these two pastorals, Wordsworth explains to Fox, were "Written with a view to shew that men who do not wear fine cloaths can feel deeply." The protagonists in "The Brothers" and "Michael" differ from such characters as Martha Ray, Simon Lee, and others in the 1798 *Lyrical Ballads*. Their feelings, unlike those of the deranged or servile characters of the earlier poems, are based on an honest confrontation of life's tragic inconstancy. And their feelings run deep because they are held bravely under control. The protagonists are also different from the conventional representation of country persons, which before Wordsworth's time had exaggerated the differences that separated man from man. In "The Brothers" and "Michael," the poet rejects the fanciful Arcadian characters of make-believe pastorals and establishes in their place real rural people who are elevated by their possession of property.

"The Brothers"—"that model of English pastoral," as Coleridge called it—is based on a story told to Wordsworth at Ennerdale. The tragic separation of two brothers is prefigured in the poem in terms of a symbolic landscape:

> On that tall pike . . .
> There were two springs which bubbled side by side,
> As if they had been made that they might be
> Companions for each other: the huge crag
> Was rent with lightning—one hath disappeared;
> The other, left behind, is flowing still.

Leonard Ewbank, after twenty years at sea, has returned to his paternal home with the determined purpose of resuming the shepherd's life he had formerly shared with his brother but had left. He meets and recognizes the village priest, but is unrecognized by him, and engages him in conversation. He learns that his brother, who was never so robust and hearty as himself, had one May day gone up the hills to look after the newborn lambs. Being wearied with the climb, he had stopped to rest on a high crag and had fallen asleep there. Upon walking in his sleep he apparently plunged to his death, for the next morning his crushed body was found on the rocks below. Leonard is so overwhelmed by the story of his brother's death that he cannot trust himself to tell the pastor who he is, but he writes him a letter that night on his way back to the seacoast to beg his understanding and forgiveness. His bonds with the community are now broken. He cannot bear now to think of returning to live in the vale.

By restrained language and tragic irony, imaginatively supported by dramatic symbolism, Wordsworth gives this simple tale a pathos that is akin to that in Greek tragedy. He convincingly makes his point that "men who do not wear fine cloaths can feel deeply."

"Michael" is a blending of two local traditions: one involves the character of Luke founded on the story of the son of an old couple who leaves home and takes to evil ways; the other centers on the person of Michael himself drawn from an old shepherd who had been seven years building a sheepfold in a solitary valley. Shepherds, Wordsworth tells us in *The Prelude* (book 8: 215–327), had been the first men to arrest his interest and admiration. In the introductory lines to "Michael" he says that such a story as that of Michael had been known to him in boyhood and "led me on to feel/For passions that were not my own, and think . . ./On man, the heart of man, and human life." Into "Michael" he poured all his faith in the shepherds of the fells whom in boyhood he had loved. Wordsworth stated in a letter to Poole that his aim in the poem was "to give a picture of a man, of strong mind and lively sensibility, agitated by two of the most powerful affections of the human heart; the parental affection, and the love of property, *landed* property, including the feelings of inheritance, home, and personal and family independence."[4]

At the opening of the poem, the reader is invited to turn his steps "up the tumultuous brook of Greenhead Ghyll" until he comes to a hidden mountain valley where beside the brook appears "a straggling heap of stones." These stones mark the site of a covenant. In them is symbolically merged the love of the land and the love for his son that were bound together in the heart of an old shepherd. The poet will relate his story, "a history homely and rude" for "the delight of a few natural hearts" and "for the sake/Of youthful Poets, who among these hills/Will be my second self when I am gone."

The shepherd Michael is the grandest character that Wordsworth ever drew. He was an old man, past eighty, but stout of heart, strong of limb, and keen of mind—more prompt and watchful in his shepherd's calling than ordinary men. From confronting the challenge of nature, he had built his strength. He had learned the meaning of all winds; and oftentimes, when others paid no heed, he heard the warning in the blasts that summoned him up the mountain. He had kept watch alone "Amid the heart of many thousand mists,/That came to him, and left him, on the heights." Over the years the fields and hills of his domain had impressed many incidents upon his mind "Of hardship, skill or courage, joy or fear." So there was built within Michael a deep and enduring attachment to the land:

> Those fields, those hills—what could they less? had laid
> Strong hold on his affections, were to him
> A pleasurable feeling of blind love,
> The pleasure which there is in life itself.

Michael was joined in his labors by a "comely matron," twenty years younger than himself; and to them an only son was born when Michael, in shepherd's phrase, had "one foot in the grave." This son, named Luke, with two brave sheepdogs, made all their household. It was a home known throughout the vale for endless industry. After the day's work was done, the housewife lighted a lamp by the light of which the couple and Luke worked at domestic tasks far into the night. The light, famous in the neighborhood, became "a public symbol of the life/That thrifty Pair had lived." The house itself was named the Evening Star.

Michael loved his helpmate, but he loved even more the son of his old age. While Luke was but an infant, the shepherd joyed to have the young one in his sight when he worked in the field or sheared the sheep near their cottage under the large oak tree, named the Clipping Tree. As the child grew, Michael saw that his son lacked no "pleasure that a boy can know." With his own hand he cut a sapling and made it into the shepherd's staff for the boy as a mark of new dignity. When the lad was ten, he stood against the mountain blasts with his father and fearlessly shared the dangers and the toil of his work. Small wonder that the objects the shepherd loved were dearer still and that responses from the boy made the old man's heart seem born again. When Luke had reached his eighteenth year, he was his father's "comfort and his daily hope."

So the simple household lived from day to day, when to Michael suddenly came distressful news. Through no fault of his own, the shepherd was called upon to pay an unlooked-for claim of nearly half his substance. His first resolve was to sell at once "a portion of his patrimonial fields," but, as he thought of his lifelong diligence to possess the land and of his purpose to hand it on to Luke to possess "free as is the wind/That passes over it," his heart failed him. To save the land it would be better, he thought, to have Luke go to the city to work and with thrift quickly pay off the debt and return. Isabel was not so sure and for a time withheld approval. The dialogue of Michael and Isabel, with its anxious probing of Michael's dilemma, is among the finest that Wordsworth ever wrote. The words, which come straight from the hearts of Michael and his wife, are a poignant revelation of their glowing hopes and cautious fears. At length, after many misgivings, Isabel agrees that Luke should go.

Before word of his disastrous loss had come to Michael, he had planned to build a sheepfold and for that purpose had gathered a heap of stones. To that spot on the evening before Luke left for the city the old man and his son repaired. There Michael asked Luke to lay one stone. And if evil men are ever his son's companions, he said, "think of me, my Son,/And of this moment; . . . a covenant/'Twill be between us." Luke stooped down and did as his father had requested: "At the sight/The Old Man's grief broke from him; to his heart/He pressed his Son, he kissèd him and wept."

The next day Luke went to the city, and at first all was well; but at length he gave himself to evil ways and was driven at last "to seeking a hiding-place beyond the seas." The son's default is treated briefly and quietly, for "Michael" is the story of the old shepherd. After Luke's defection, one might think that the old man would be crushed with grief and die. He suffered, but he did so bravely, and through his love of Luke his heart was born again:

> There is comfort in the strength of love;
> 'Twill make a thing endurable, which else
> Would overset the brain, or break the heart . . .
> And to that hollow dell from time to time
> Did he repair to build the Fold of which
> His flock had need. 'Tis not forgotten yet
> The pity which was then in every heart

> For the old Man—and 'tis believed by all
> That many and many a day he thither went,
> And never lifted up a single stone.

In Michael, there is concentrated the patient strength of a man who has lived "in the strength of nature." With strange and lonely fidelity he still looked up to sun and cloud and went about his work for "the length of full seven years." But, when he died, he left the sheepfold unfinished. The land was sold and went into a stranger's hand. The cottage, named by men the Evening Star, is gone. Only the great oak beside the door remained as a reminder of that house of industry. And on the mountain side the pile of rocks lies untouched, a poignant talisman of Michael's tragedy.

"Michael" is one of the best-loved of all Wordsworth's writings. The story draws close to a kind of loss and suffering that occurs in some form to everyone. The tale is told as one coming from the people, as one "believed by all." The poet is the communal spokesman. Yet the pathos that pervades the poem arises from the poet's making a common story completely his own by creating a sympathetic persona and speaking with sheer, penetrating power. The diction is pure and natural; colloquial phrases are touched with a dignity that gives them universal appeal. Simple statements of thought and feeling are given profound significance. They move to the ethical discovery, central in Wordsworth's moral teaching, "that suffering, when illuminated by love, creates its own nobility of heart."[5]

Preface to *Lyrical Ballads,* 1800 and 1802

The poems written in Germany and during the first year at Grasmere were gathered together for a second volume to *Lyrical Ballads* and were published with a Preface in 1800. The chief instigator of the Preface was Coleridge; however, the Preface was emphatically Wordsworth's composition and contained some opinions that Coleridge did not share. Years later Coleridge wrote a critique of it spelling out his points of disagreement with Wordsworth's style in poetry and with his ideas. Even at the time, Coleridge was conscious of certain conflicts that by 1802 made him "suspect that somewhere there is a *radical* difference in our theoretical opinions respecting poetry."[6] The differences, however, could not have been truly radical, for they seem to have shared the basic literary principles of the central tradition begun by Aristotle: both subscribe in their central theoretical works to his principles and refer to him by name.[7]

Wordsworth's place in the history of literary theory has nevertheless been an issue long in dispute. A long-standing view, in fact, is that Wordsworth was a major participant in a "Romantic Revolution," a cataclysmic break in literary theory occurring some time near the year 1800. M. H. Abrams, lately most closely associated with such a view, helped the view along by attempting to give it a more solid theoretical basis.[8] Abrams first pointed to the fountain image implicit in Wordsworth's expression "all good poetry is the spontaneous overflow of powerful feelings," next linked the fountain image to other lamp images of the time, and then concluded that such images represent an expressionist view of the poet to be contrasted with the traditional mimetic view represented by the traditional image of a mirror held up to nature. Abrams thus placed Wordsworth among the new expressionists, even though Abrams qualifies this claim several times in footnote references to Wordsworth's clearly traditional principles.

A new view agrees with the footnote qualifications of Abrams rather than with his central claim and makes a strong case for Wordsworth as indeed traditional. In the Preface to *Lyrical Ballads,* the major text, Wordsworth seems to consider mimesis, the truthful representation of human experience, to be self-evident: "Poetry is the image of man and nature." And he follows tradition by qualifying this representation in the direction of the general or universal: "Aristotle, I have been told, has said that Poetry is the most philosophic of all writing: it is so: its object is truth, not individual and local, but general. . . ." Wordsworth's basic allegiance appears to be unmistakable; he certainly seems, here and elsewhere, to feel himself a member of a tradition.

Traditions that are vital, however, always accommodate change, and Wordsworth made the single most important revision in the theory of the central tradition when he proposed a change in the way morality was seen to work since the time of Horace. The traditional view—that literature taught morality by precept and example—was rather crude. This view Wordsworth replaced with one of indirection: "[Poets] describe objects, and utter sentiments, of such a nature, and in such connection with each other, that the understanding of the Reader must necessarily be in some degree enlightened, and his affections strengthened and purified." By telling the truth about human experience and by showing in the process how to feel about it, literature prepares the reader to be a more aware and sensitive moral agent. Such a view can also be found in several letters and in other of Wordsworth's more formal works of theory, and it is expanded upon later by Matthew Arnold, the next major theorist in the tradition.[9]

Wordsworth's mention of literature's ability to strengthen and purify the reader's emotions can be seen as part of his concern about what he saw as the emotional corruption of the times: "For a multitude of causes, unknown to former times, are now acting with a combined force to blunt the discriminating powers of the mind, and, unfitting it for all voluntary exertion, to reduce it to a state of almost savage torpor." Healthy feelings can no longer be taken for granted, neither the reader's nor the poet's.

Concern for the poet may be part of the reason Wordsworth turned some of his attention to creative theory, although in the eighteenth century there was already considerable interest being shown in how literature is created in the writer's mind. In any case, the following famous passage in the Preface helps to explain Abrams's ready identification of Wordsworth as an expressionist: "Poetry is the spontaneous overflow of powerful feelings: it takes its origin from emotion recollected in tranquillity: the emotion is contemplated till, by a species of re-action, the tranquillity gradually disappears, and an emotion, kindred to that which was before the subject of contemplation, is gradually produced, and does itself actually exist in the mind. In this mood successful composition generally begins." This passage of *creative* theory, however, contains nothing that is incompatible with traditional *literary* theory. That is, poetry can still be mimetic and universal regardless of its genesis within the poet.

Wordsworth's interest in creative theory is again shown in his preface to *Collected Poems* (1815), where imagination replaces feeling as the dominant factor, much as it is seen by Samuel Taylor Coleridge in his *Biographia Literaria* (1817). Neither is very clear in his attempts at defining the imagination; save for some explicit disagreements, however, they do tend to agree.

Beyond such basic literary and creative theory, Wordsworth in the Preface to *Lyrical Ballads* dealt with more specific theory of content and form. He first considered subject matter, opening it up by offering a new way of considering it. He overturned the traditional consideration of decorum of genre—that, for example, a high genre required a high style—by ignoring genre altogether in the Preface; instead he offered a new formula: "The feeling therein developed [in his poems] gives importance to the action and situation, and not the action and situation to the feeling." It was natural for Wordsworth to use the traditional ballad form to introduce this formula, for the ballad had long treated elemental subjects in what was considered a low style.

Then Wordsworth turned directly to style itself, especially diction, for by the eighteenth century a high style with a whole set of mannerisms had developed as the style appropriate, according to decorum, for the high genres. Wordsworth in the Preface mentioned only personifications, but he had in mind a larger set of conventions he called "the family language" of poets, which he rejected altogether. If he had simply listed the sort of thing he rejected, such as compound epithets and circumlocutions, rather than attempt to offer a set of positive phrasings, such as "the real language of men" and "the language of prose when prose is well written," he might perhaps have stirred up less controversy.

The Preface to *Lyrical Ballads* and Wordsworth's literary criticism as a whole had a large impact. The literary theory changed the way the central tradition looked at literature as a moral force. And his other, more specific pronouncements on subject matter and style affected the way poetry would be written in the future. Especially in the twentieth century the choice of subject matter in poetry widened immensely and was conveyed in a much less exclusive diction.

Chapter Four
The Prelude

The year 1798 was one of widespread pessimism in England: the conservatives were scornful of utopian dreams, and the reformers were disillusioned about chances of improving society; the war with France had reached a state of crisis. In the midst of this national gloom, Wordsworth, who had recovered from his own disenchantment with political chimeras, was eager to share with others a way of regaining hope and peace of soul. Early in March, spurred by Coleridge's enthusiasm, he undertook a long philosophical poem, which he hoped "to make of considerable utility," to be entitled *The Recluse; or, Views on Man, on Nature, and on Human Life.*

Wordsworth launched into his new undertaking with high spirits; but, after turning out several hundred lines, he was overwhelmed with doubts about his ability to carry through the tremendous task he had set for himself. He decided he should review his powers to determine "how far nature and education had qualified him to construct a literary work that might live." The result of this self-examination was *The Prelude*. It was Wordsworth's intention to make *The Prelude* introductory to *The Recluse;* but, because the new poem far outran the original scheme, ultimately reaching the great length of fourteen books and better than eight thousand lines, it was deemed not suitable for that purpose. However, *The Prelude* stands independently as an account of the origin and development of the poetic mind and as the most vital work of Wordsworth's genius.

At Goslar in the winter of 1798–99 Wordsworth set to work in earnest on the poem of his early life by recalling all that nature had done for him in childhood. The lines he then wrote make up the better part of book 1 and include parts of books 5 and 12. After his return to England in May 1799, the inspiration came to him to dedicate to Coleridge the poem now shaping in his mind. The dedication to his friend was a great incitement; without it, he might not have been able to carry the poem through to completion. For Coleridge was the friend of Wordsworth's genius as well as of his heart, a fact underscored throughout *The Prelude*. Probably at some point during the summer of 1799 book 2 was composed.

However, after Wordsworth moved into Dove Cottage in December

1799, he could not progress with his poem. Instead, much to Coleridge's disappointment, Wordsworth occupied himself composing sonnets and other short pieces. At last, in the fall of 1803, he roused himself again to the task and seems to have written in some coherent form the preamble and postpreamble (the first 271 lines of book 1). In the spring of 1804, under the stimulus of Coleridge's departure for Malta, Wordsworth turned again to the poem's composition and completed it through book 5. At this time he altered his plan for ending his self-examination with the dedication to poetry in his nineteenth year to the fuller project of a poem that would include his experience in France and bring the story down to 1798, when he felt his powers were matured and ready for expression. This called for eight more books after the fifth, all of which were brought to completion in June 1805.

The finished work fell far short of what Wordsworth had seemed capable of achieving. Partly for this reason and partly because it was a highly personal document, publication was withheld until after his death. But it was not laid aside and forgotten; often during the next thirty-five years he returned to *The Prelude* to revise it. The poem published in 1850 differs widely, therefore, from the one completed in 1805, and most often editions print both versions. Wordsworth had given it no title: it was known to his family and friends as "the poem to Coleridge" or as "the poem on his own early life." For its publication, Mary Wordsworth most appropriately chose *The Prelude* as its title.

Synopsis

The Prelude opens with the recording of a joyous hymn, the so-called glad preamble, chanted by the poet to render thanks for his release from the bondage of the city. As the wind was blowing on his body, he felt within the breath of creative inspiration and was buoyed up with "A chearful confidence in things to come." After the spontaneous self-dedication, according to the next two hundred and fifty lines, he relaxed into passive contentment; contemplated various themes for a great work; was overcome with indecision; and, finally baffled by his inability to compose, fell into a mood of morbid introspection and despair. Was it for a bafflement such as this, he asked himself, that the river Derwent had nourished him in childhood?

The poem properly begins with an account of the twofold discipline he had received from nature: "Fair seed-time had my soul, and I grew up/ Foster'd alike by beauty and by fear." Adventures from school days at Hawkshead through his twelfth year, which contributed ultimately to his poetic power, are recounted. These include such "incidents of fear" as his theft of a woodcock from another's trapline, the plundering of raven's eggs on the high crag, and the "severer intervention" of nature's discipline when he stole a boat in the darkness. Then it was that a huge cliff "like a living thing" strode after him and for days "huge and mighty Forms" troubled his dreams. More quietly he tells of the ministry of beauty: when he was skating, "the stars Eastward were sparkling clear"; at other times, how he would drink in "a pure organic pleasure" from the beauty "of curling mist" or from "the level plain/Of waters colour'd by the steady clouds."

Book 2 traces the poet's development from unconscious intercourse with nature, as set forth in book 1, to an active awareness of "the sentiment of Being." The schoolboy episodes in the earlier part (to line 203) are intermediate, and the period covered in this section is from Wordsworth's thirteenth to his fifteenth year. During this time, while engaged in boyish sports among scenes of natural beauty, nature was revealed collaterally. For example, the poet tells how, on an excursion to Furness Abbey, when with glee he and his companions were racing their horses through the chantry, he heard the singing of an invisible wren and was filled with a poignant desire to remain in that place forever "to hear such music."

With line 203, a new stage in Wordsworth's development commences. Beginning in his fifteenth and lasting until his seventeenth year, he relates how nature was sought for her own sake. From boyish play, he turned to solitude, passionate friendship, vague yearnings and idealism, and the unutterable thoughts of youth. To "Nature's finer influxes" his mind then lay open, and he thrilled to discover in objects the manifold affinities not seen by others. On early morning walks alone among the hills he experienced moments of mystic calm, spiritual closeness to nature, and a consciousness of "plastic power" within him. He had received so much from nature that all his thoughts "were steep'd in feeling." In all things he "saw one life, and felt that it was joy." He laments the defection of those who have lost faith in mankind, and he concludes with an affectionate address to Coleridge, who, though reared in the city, has come to share his own deep devotion to nature.

Book 3 tells of Wordsworth's first year at St. John's College, Cambridge. Upon his arrival, he was in high spirits and moved easily into the strange, motley world around him. Yet he had little regard for the program of college studies and had doubts about the reasons for his being there. When he was alone, he sensed a deep and quiet mental strength within himself. At times, he felt a spiritual contact with the illustrious poets who had preceded him at Cambridge—Chaucer, Spenser, and Milton. Mostly, he spent the year in a mixed round of social idleness and in halfhearted accession to academic duty. He did not find there the love of learning that should possess youth. How different, he thought, it must have been with the medieval lovers of truth who had resided at Cambridge. The year in retrospect seemed like a day at a museum: he suffered a barren sense of gay confusion, but something was left in the memory for future use.

Book 4 begins in a joyous mood with the college youth on the heights overlooking Lake Windermere on his way back to Hawkshead for his first summer vacation. He had glad greetings from all the villagers and from old Dame Tyson, to whose memory Wordsworth pays a fine tribute. He experienced great happiness in seeing the throng of familiar things about the cottage that had been his home, and at night he especially enjoyed lying down again upon the bed where he had so often heard the roaring wind and clamorous rain and had watched "The moon in splendour couch'd among the leaves/Of a tall ash." Freed now from the confinement of college life, the poet tells with gratitude of how he returned to his solitary walks and how, on making again the familiar circuit of Esthwaite Lake, he was lifted into suprasensuous communion: "Gently did my soul/ Put off her veil, and self-transmuted, stood/Naked as in the presence of her God." Trivial vanities often intervened to stop the course of lofty contemplation. But on one memorable occasion, when he was returning home alone after a night of revelry, the radiant beauty of the dawn so exalted him that he was filled with a sense of solemn dedication. During this summer vacation, Wordsworth was also awakened to a new awareness of the worth and simple goodness of the plain-living country people: "With another eye," he says, "I saw the quiet Woodman in the Woods,/The Shepherd on the Hills." Book 4 closes with an account of his surprise encounter in the darkness with an "uncouth shape," a vagrant soldier whom he befriended and aided.

Book 5 relates what Wordsworth owed to books in early life. It opens with the lament that consecrated books, worthy to endure forever, must perish. Related to this disconsolate thought is the nightmarish dream about an Arab intent upon carrying off all learning. The dreamer, who had been reading *Don Quixote* by the sea, fell into a sleep and dreamed. In his dream he was joined by an Arab mounted upon his dromedary bearing underneath one arm a stone (mathematics) and in the opposite hand a shining shell (poetry). From the shell there came a prophecy foretelling the destruction of the earth by deluge. On learning this forecast, the Arab moved forward rapidly across the desert intent on burying his two books; and the dreamer followed him. When a glittering light revealed the waters of the deep advancing upon them, the Arab quickened his pace and was last seen "With the fleet waters of the drowning world/In chase of him." The dreamer woke in terror. Wordsworth sympathizes with the Arab's anxiety, for great books are powers only less than nature's self. He is grateful for the freedom allowed him as a schoolboy to roam widely in his reading rather than being confined by careful tutoring. In a satiric vein, he launches into an attack upon the child prodigy stuffed with false learning by the disciples of Jean Jacques Rousseau's *Émile*. To Wordsworth, it would be better to let the old fairy tales and romances, the rough and tumble of the schoolyard, and the secret ministries of nature join in making their influence felt in shaping "A race of real children, not too wise,/Too learned, or too good." His own special treasure as a schoolboy was the *Arabian Nights,* which satisfied his "cravings for the marvelous." When he reached his early teens, the charm of romance yielded to the love of poetry, in which he found a sweet satisfaction, "a passion and a power." He concludes with an apology for omitting to say anything about the influence of books in his later years, but such acknowledgment he never made.

Book 6 treats casually his second and third years at Cambridge without differentiating between them. Wordsworth lived more to himself and settled into more promising habits, but he continued to be indifferent to the prescribed course of study. Indeed, his summer vacations offered the most rewarding experiences during these years, the first of which was spent in the Lake Country in the company of his sister Dorothy and Mary Hutchinson. As he recalls that summer, the poet feels a strong inclination to add Coleridge to the group, though then unknown to them, and he pays a glowing tribute to his genius. The third summer vacation spent with his college mate, Robert Jones, on a walking tour of the Swiss and Italian Alps was truly a glorious, memorable adventure—one richly rewarding to him as a poet.

Book 7 blends the experiences of two periods of residence in London: the first period subsequent to his graduation from college; the second, following his return from France. Before he ever went to the city, Wordsworth's youthful fancy had shaped marvelous visions of the wonders to be seen there. These gave way in due season, and when he went to live intimately day by day in the motley, bustling metropolis, his keen and lively pleasures were intermixed with disappointments. He roamed·the streets, watched intently the street entertainments, and beheld in the crowds "all specimens of Man." He enjoyed spectacles within doors: art galleries, pantomimic shows, melodrama at Sadler's Wells, and more solid entertainment at the theaters. He was distressed to see an innocent child surrounded by dissolute, debased humanity. A blind beggar with a sign became for him the symbol of "the utmost that we know,/Both of ourselves and of the universe." With a touch of satire he portrays the young politician displaying his oratorical powers and the bachelor preacher winding "through many a maze,/A minuet course." In striking contrast with the daytime bustle is London at night in solemn calmness, beauty, and peace. Though blank confusion wearies the eye, there is in the city, to him who looks in steadiness, amidst "the press/Of self-destroying, transitory things/Composure and ennobling Harmony."

Book 8 reviews the steps that led Wordsworth not only to the love of nature but ultimately to the love of mankind. Man is brought into the ominous presence of nature in a small gathering of country people holding a summer festival on the side of Mount Helvellyn. "How little They, they and their doings seem,/ . . . and yet how great!" The nobility of man had early been impressed upon the boy Wordsworth through his admiration of the shepherds in the mountains. Their domain was more beautiful by far than any legendary paradise, and their life, fraught with danger and distress, was more noble than any other. With his concept of man thus exalted, Wordsworth, when confronted by wretchedness and vice in the city, remained steadfast in his trust in "Man ennobled."

But the love of man was not predominant until the poet's twenty-second year. He reviews the growth of his love of nature from the early years when it was secondary to his "own pursuits and animal activities," through the period of his youth when "wilful Fancy" fictionized natural objects, to "the time of greater dignity" when he felt "The pulse of Being everywhere, . . . One galaxy of life and joy." "Then rose Man, . . . as of all visible natures crown." In the city of London, that "Fountain of my Country's destiny," he felt most intensely the spiritual essence of human nature. The city was "thronged with impregnations" and "Affectingly set forth, more than elsewhere/Is possible, the unity of man." Nature led him by slow gradations until the poet was independently established in his love of humankind.

In Book 9, Wordsworth says he went to France chiefly to learn the language, and for that purpose he chose to live in Orleans. On his way there he stopped for a few days in Paris and visited the sites made memorable by the revolution, but he did not feel emotionally involved. At Orleans, he was at first content to be a spectator; however, it was not long before he was won over to the revolutionary cause. The chief instrument in bringing about his conversion was, as has been noted, Michel Beaupuy, a royalist military officer who had turned patriot. Wordsworth had been bred up to democratic ways both at Hawkshead and afterward at Cambridge; therefore, the

French Revolution "Seemed nothing out of nature's certain course." Hence, Beaupuy, who became Wordsworth's close companion, found him a ready convert. The patriot's arguments received firm intellectual support from the French revolutionary philosophers and from that handbook of all good democrats, Plutarch's *Lives*. Wordsworth's conversion was emotionally confirmed when the two companions one day met a hunger-bitten victim of oppression and his friend excitedly said, "'Tis against *that*/that we are fighting." The remainder of book 9 is devoted to the tragic love story of Vaudracour and Julia, a fictionalized account of Wordsworth's own affair with Annette Vallon. This recital was removed from *The Prelude* as hindering the forward motion of its central theme and published separately.

In book 10, the poet has arrived in Paris on his way back to England and shortly after the September massacres. He ranged the city as he had before but more eagerly, and as he lay on his bed at night he felt "a substantial dread" and was filled with gloomy forebodings. During his time there, the extremist Robespierre gained ascendancy, and Wordsworth inwardly prayed that a great leader of moderate temper might rise to lead the nation. Reluctantly, he returned home, but he was full of hope for France and for the cause of universal liberty among all peoples. When England's declaration of war on France suddenly came, Wordsworth was shocked to his deepest self; he felt that the war was both a tragedy and a blunder. Although the senseless slaughter of the Reign of Terror filled the poet with despair, he rationalized it as the necessary consequence of a reservoir of guilt "That could no longer hold its loathsome charge." A great lift was given to his spirit one summer evening at Leven's estuary following a visit to the grave of his schoolmaster, William Taylor, when, from a casual inquiry of a traveler, he received the stirring reply that *Robespierre was dead*. Filled with great joy, he pursued his way along the very sands upon which as a boy he had "in wantonness of heart" raced his horse with his schoolmates.

In book 10 (book 11 of the final version), Wordsworth has kept faith with the ability of the people of France to settle their internal dissensions and to triumph over their enemies. He recalls with fervor how his own ideals for mankind were given strong support during the early years of the republic: "Bliss was it in that dawn to be alive,/But to be young was very heaven." The whole earth then wore the promise of happiness such as one dreams of in a utopia, but this dream was now to be realized in the very world in which he lived. Even when Frenchmen engaged in excesses, the poet excused them on the grounds "That throwing off oppression must be the work/As well of license as of liberty."

When England challenged France with open war, his pride in his own country turned to shame. Subsequently, when France "changed a war of self-defence/For one of conquest," he still held stubbornly to his early belief in her cause. But strong emotional ties to his own country finally trapped Wordsworth in a conflict of allegiances from which he retreated to an illusion of security in the rational philosophy of Godwin. Following Godwin's lead, he dreamed that social freedom could be built upon that of independent intellect. It was not long before his speculations lured him into an intricate maze of contradictions, until, demanding *proof* and "wearied out with contrarieties," he "Yielded up moral questions in despair." At this juncture Coleridge, Dorothy, and "Nature's Self" helped to guide him back to his true self. Dorothy, in the midst of all, preserved him "still a Poet." Wordsworth closes the lengthy survey of his response to public events with an affectionate address to Coleridge, who is in Sicily, and he offers a devoted wish that his friend may there be restored to good health.

In book 11 (book 12 in 1850), Wordsworth reviews the period during which he became an idolater of analytical reason. At that time even nature was not immune from contamination by his presumptuous habit of judging. He followed the "cult of the picturesque" in comparing scene with scene and in pampering himself "with meagre novelties/Of colour and proportion." Insatiably, he sought delights that pleased the sight, but not the mind. How different was his sister Dorothy's converse with nature! Without intermeddling questioning, whatever scene she looked on yielded a sweetness that bespoke her own sweet presence. So it was with Dorothy's freedom of spirit that Wordsworth worshiped nature in his early years among his native hills and so it was when he roamed through the Alps. But force of custom or aggravation of the times dulled his once vibrant communion with nature. At last he shook off the stultifying habit of analysis and again stood in nature's presence "A sensitive and a creative soul." Our minds, he explains, are from early childhood nourished and invisibly repaired by "spots of time." He tells of two such "spots," one near Penrith Beacon when he had become half-faint with terror at the sight of initials carved in the turf marking the place where a murderer had been hanged; the other at his father's funeral (December 1783), when he remembered his own trivial expectancy in anticipation of the Christmas holidays.

In book 12 (13 in 1850), Wordsworth, restored to right reason and creative power, has found "once more in Man an object of delight." Sanguine schemes pleased him less, and he looked inquiringly at what makes the dignity of individual man. Why is it, he asks, that "This glorious Creature" is to be found "One only in ten thousand?" To discover man as he really is, the poet turned to the public roads to watch and question those he met and to hold familiar talk with them. Because his faith in rural life to breed a good life was strengthened, he decided that simple, country folk would be the substance of his poetry.

Wordsworth was convinced that nature had a power to shape the inner being of man and that each poet especially has his peculiar dower by which "he is enabled to perceive/Something unseen before" and from that influx create something that might become "a power like one of Nature's." To such a mood, he says, he was once lifted during a walk upon the Plain of Sarum when in vision he saw the primitive Britons offering living sacrifices on their altars. On his lonesome journey he composed a poem of familiar, everyday affairs ("The Female Vagrant") into which—so Coleridge said—he infused touches of a higher power. Perhaps Coleridge's approval was a judgment biased by friendship. Nevertheless, Wordsworth remembers well that he seemed at that time to have sight of a new world, one fit to be recorded in verse for all to share.

Book 13 (book 14), the last book, centers on Wordsworth's excursion with his friend Jones and a guide up Mount Snowdon on a murky summer's night to see the sunrise from the top. During the ascent, the sky was low-hung with clouds that threatened rain; the climbers, hemmed in by fog and damp, could see nothing around them. Then, with the poet in the lead, the ground began to brighten as they neared the top; he instantly looked up to see the moon standing "naked in the Heavens." At his feet extended a huge sea of mist upon which the moon shone in single glory. Some distance away there was a break in the mist, "a deep and gloomy breathing-place," through which the roar of innumerable waters mounted as with one voice.

To Wordsworth, this majestic scene, with nature making the mist appear first to be water and then land, was the perfect image of the poetic mind when actively possessed with creative power. This faculty, imagination, is the highest power that man may know, for it allows him to see the visionary unity of all things. Wordsworth rounds out his recital with sincere and affectionate tributes to Dorothy and to Coleridge for the roles they played in shaping a poet's mind. He concludes with a prayerful wish that he may have "a few short years" in which to write poetry that will teach men to love what he and Coleridge have learned to love.

To a considerable extent *The Prelude* is autobiographical; but it obviously is not merely a narrative of the first twenty-seven years of its author's life. Wordsworth makes no attempt to give a faithful account of external happenings.[1] Purely personal events are twisted out of normal order; some are omitted, and others are simplified so that the essential truth may be presented more clearly. Sometimes the facts of his life are completely ignored.

Wordsworth is not so much telling the story of his life as recounting the rich imaginative experiences that were his; he is tracing the steps by which the mind absorbed and reshaped external circumstances until self-knowledge and imaginative power were attained.

The Prelude's greatness does not consist, therefore, in its biographical accuracy. It is an idealization, not a factual rendering, of the poet's life. In it the author's penetration to the essential nature and power of the poetic mind transforms whatever is personal into the universal. As a balm for pessimism and a lodestar to direct his countrymen to new hope, The Prelude tells how a poet acquired true knowledge and, when he was led astray, how his flagging spirit was resuscitated. In the early books, nature is shown as playing the leading role in awakening and instructing his faculties. In the middle books, he exposes himself as a prodigal from nature, betrayed by rationality. In the last books, he shows how imaginative power was restored and he became "a sensitive and creative soul" dedicated to the universal heart of man.

Themes and Ideas

The Prelude was not carefully thought out in advance. As it progressed, there were shifts in direction; and secondary materials were added that seem unrelated to the central theme. The initial purpose may be surmised from the famous section highly praised by Coleridge, "Wisdom and Spirit of the Universe" (book 1, 428–41),[2] first published in The Friend under the title "Growth of Genius from the Influence of Natural Objects on the Imagination in Boyhood and Early Youth." Throughout books 1 and 2 the emphasis is on the power of imagination to transform simple incidents. In the four years that passed after the completion of the second book, Wordsworth grew in the understanding of his objective. When he moved into the composition of the third book, he realized that the poem's real center, its unifying principle, was to be found in the imagination. Perhaps nowhere in the works of Wordsworth does the poetic passion burn with a purer flame than when he contemplates in this book the exalted role of imagination and the epical grandeur of the task he has set for himself:

> Of genius, power,
> Creation and divinity itself
> I have been speaking, for my theme has been
> What passed within me. Not of outward things
> Done visibly for other minds, words, signs,

> Symbols or actions, but of my own heart
> Have I been speaking, and my youthful mind.
> O Heavens! how awful is the might of souls,
> And what they do within themselves while yet
> The yoke of earth is new to them, the world
> Nothing but a wild field where they were sown.
> This is, in truth, heroic argument,
> And genuine prowess, which I wish'd to touch
> With hand however weak, but in the main
> It lies far hidden from the reach of words.
> (1850; 3:173–87)

The faculty of imagination, the poetic faculty par excellence, becomes, then, the real hero, the presiding genius of the *The Prelude*. In the most awesome and haunting passages that tell of the imagination (as in the sixth book following the narrative of the travelers' crossing of the Alps), the poet reveals how this power has brought him to "the highest bliss/ That can be known." By means of it, the invisible is revealed to him, and beauty is transmuted into truth. Imagination finally leads to a moral victory for the poet in the attainment of intellectual love. In the process of acquiring imagination, no one can help another, but nature can and does assist—as Wordsworth demonstrates throughout the poem. To follow his demonstration, one needs to understand what Wordsworth means by nature.

Partly as a result of happy childhood associations and partly as a result of ideas inherited from the eighteenth-century Deists, Wordsworth developed a faith in the beneficent power of nature. Like the Deists, he held that God revealed himself in the beauties and sublimities of untamed nature. Like them, he believed that the natural world is the expression of divine wisdom with a view to the well-being of the whole of creation and of mankind in particular. But, unlike his eighteenth-century predecessors, Wordsworth brought the Creator from His far-off heaven to inhabit this very present world. He was conscious of an animating spirit moving through all nature with a shaping power, a drive, and directive force. As he put it in "Tintern Abbey," he felt a presence "far more deeply interfused,"

> Whose dwelling is the light of setting suns
> And the round ocean and the living air,
> And the blue sky, and in the mind of man:

A motion and a spirit, that impels
All thinking things, all objects of all thought,
And rolls through all things.

The animating principle of universal nature Wordsworth identifies with deity, but he is chary during the years 1797 to 1805 of using the word "God." There are a good many passages in *The Prelude* that suggest an approximation to pantheism (the belief that the universe is God and God is the universe, so that, if it were destroyed, He would no longer exist). But, for the most part, Wordsworth dismisses any literal pantheistic identification of the spirit life with the sum of physical things. Perhaps a better term to describe his idea of nature is *panentheistic,* for he believed in a power that was both within and beyond earthly forms, a power within but also "far more deeply interfused." His representation of the spirituality of nature is varied and free; for example, he repeatedly expresses a belief that there are spirits or tutelary powers who inhabit the solitudes. Quite literally he means that there is "a spirit in the woods" acting under the direction of the Deity.[3] Frequently, he thought of nature as a spirit endowed with personality, a purposive intelligence who animates and guides the external world. So guided, nature by extrinsic passion peopled his mind with grand and beauteous forms and made him love them.

The most important aspect of nature for Wordsworth is the mystical belief in the "unity of all." Quite literally, God and nature are one. There is no division between man and nature and none between nature and God—all adhere in a mighty unity. "Each thing has a life of its own and we are all one life," wrote Coleridge, interpreting Spinoza. So, with Wordsworth, all forms of nature are linked into "one galaxy of life and joy." Natural objects are interpenetrative in a fluid pattern with each other and with the mind of man. There is a constant interplay of external and internal. Wordsworth felt a mysterious presence flowing through surrounding things that ministered to him, quickened his sensibilities, and assisted his meditations. He shows us in *The Prelude* how this is so. He follows the steps by which as child, as youth, and as man he is led to the great end of creation, the reproduction of creative mind, the imagination. And just as he received this triumphant ministration through nature, so, he believed, may other men receive it.

The spirit of nature permeates *The Prelude,* and it serves directly in the complex development of the human mind. Wordsworth's explanation of this development is based upon associationist theories. According to associationist psychology, human knowledge originates in perceptions made by the five senses. These perceptions through association are transformed into the aggregates of mental life. All is built up from the outside; however, from the first an activity or motion of the human spirit transmutes the mental complexes into their appropriate personal values.

Wordsworth recognized from the beginning, even in "Tintern Abbey," that sensations were informed by the creative mind. In books 1 and 2 of *The Prelude*, where associationist psychology is evident,[4] he portrays his childhood not as the period of sensations merely, but as the joyous time in which an "auxiliar light/Came from my mind," which bestowed new splendor on the external world. In these early books, Wordsworth tells of moments that transcended sense and were of a distinctly mystical quality:

> Oft in those moments such a holy calm
> Did overspread my soul, that I forgot
> That I had bodily eyes, and what I saw
> Appear'd like something in myself, a dream,
> A prospect in my mind.[5]
>
> (2:367–71)

By the time he began the composition of book 3 in 1803 a philosophy had emerged that was distinctly intuitionist. The mighty world of eye and ear became less important than the mightier one of the mind. In the last books of *The Prelude* Wordsworth identifies as paramount in the molding of personality a transcendental faculty derived from a suprapersonal agency communicating its message to consciousness:

> This efficacious spirit chiefly lurks
> Among those passages of life in which
> We have had deepest feeling that the mind
> Is lord and master, and that outward sense
> Is but the obedient servant of her will.
>
> (11:269–73)

The great paradox of Wordsworth is his simultaneous attachment to the senses and his need for a higher faculty that synthesizes, transfuses, and modifies experience. The poet gives great weight to the role of sensory factors in knowledge because he realizes "how exquisitely the external World is fitted to the Mind." But in *The Prelude* he far overreaches associationist mechanism by supplying a transcendental activity of the mind. This inward mental creativeness vitalizes the report of the senses and adds an imperisha-

ble increment of power to existence. This creative power Wordsworth identifies as imagination.

Wordsworth has an exalted concept of imagination. In book 13 (168–
70), he says that imagination "Is but another name for absolute strength/
And clearest insight, amplitude of mind,/And reason in her most exalted
mood." So Wordsworth defines imagination, but the transcendent experience of it he was never able to describe; for it is not only ineffable but ultimately incomprehensible. No passage better illustrates the recondite
mystery that confronted him than the one in book 6 where he recounts the
adventure in crossing the Alps. At the climax of his recital, imagination
lifted itself "like an unfather'd vapour" and halted his effort to continue.
When he recovered and could go on, he recognized but could not describe
the glory of that usurpation:

> To my Soul I say
> I recognize thy glory; in such strength
> Of usurpation, in such visitings
> Of awful promise, when the light of sense
> Goes out in flashes that have shewn to us
> The invisible world, doth Greatness make abode,
> There harbours whether we be young or old.
> Our destiny, our nature, and our home
> Is with infinitude, and only there.
>
> (6:531–39)

Through imagination the poet enters into communion with the invisible
world; he apprehends the infinite and becomes aware of the eternal spirit
that pervades and unifies all existence. Man himself becomes a spirit living
in time and space far diffused; man's spirit is merged with this spiritual
power, which is itself the great Imagination, World Soul, and "Reason in her
most exalted mood." To participate in the creative act of perfect self-
identification with the great imagination is to know intellectual freedom; it
is to experience the very love of God Himself.

The creative imagination works with the stuff of memory surcharged
with emotion. Visitations of this active power Wordsworth identifies as
"spots of time," and he sees them as occurring most frequently, but by no
means exclusively, in childhood. Midway in book 12, partly to explain his
restoration as "a sensitive and creative soul," he tells of "spots of time" that
in existence retain "a renovating Virtue" by which "our minds/Are nourished and invisibly repaired." At its simplest level, the "spot" is a past

event so charged and transformed that, when recalled to mind, the poet's imaginative power is revived and his moral being strengthened. This recall was not accomplished merely through mechanical recollection, but by means of the powerful emotion associated with and built upon the original experience.

In the first of the incidents recounted, the poet describes how as a child when he happened upon the site where a murderer had once been executed he fled with terror from the place. Years later this fearful adventure is refracted through another memory, a benign one. As a college youth in the company of his sister and Mary Hutchinson, he roamed about during a summer holiday "in daily presence of this very scene." By a mysterious and complex transfer of power he felt a "radiance more sublime" from the remembrances of the first terror-haunted visitation. So, Wordsworth says, "feeling comes in aid/Of feeling, and diversity of strength/Attends us, if but once we have been strong."

In another "spot of time" he tells of his turbulent impatience one Christmastime when he was waiting for the horses that were to bear him and his brothers home. Not ten days later his father died, and the boy interpreted the event as a divine chastisement provoked by his impatience. In his maturity this crude belief had long been put aside, but the mysterious occurrence, charged with emotion and touched with infinity, made it one of those "spots of time" in his childhood to which he "often would repair and thence would drink,/As at a fountain."

In book 5, in the "spot of time" involving the boy who "blew mimic hootings to the owls," which was first published separately, Wordsworth explains how nature assists in the development of imagination. He has represented in this poem, he says in the 1815 preface, "a commutation and transfer of internal feelings, cooperating with external accidents to plant, for immortality, images of sight and sound, in the celestial soil of the Imagination. The Boy, there introduced, is listening, with something of a feverish and restless anxiety, for the recurrence of the riotous sounds which he had previously excited; and, at the moment when the intenseness of his mind is beginning to remit, he is surprized into a perception of the solemn and tranquillizing images which the Poem describes." The boy's energies were braced in expectancy to hear the owls, then relaxed; and in that moment the beauty of the natural scene, falling upon his eye, carried far into his heart a sense of the enduring power of nature.[6]

In much the same way in the "spot of time" memorializing the poet's experience in the Simplon Pass, he shows how a consciousness of the terrible beauty of the mountain pass came upon him during the "dull and heavy slackening" of his feelings following the tidings of the peasant that he and his companion already "*had crossed the Alps.*" During the travelers' climb, the physical senses were pitched to high expectancy, but they failed to report what should have been the climactic moment of their adventure. It was in the slackness that ensued that the imagination fed upon the images of nature in an especially awesome setting—decaying lofty woods, waterfalls, shooting torrents, black drizzling crags, unfettered clouds—which became in recollection transformed into "symbols of Eternity,/Of first and last, and midst, and without end."

In what is usually taken to be the concluding "spot of time," the ascent of Mt. Snowdon, there is no psychological sequence of tension and remission. Wordsworth and his companions, with the poet in the lead, were making their way up the mountain in the dead of night when the ground at his feet began to brighten. He looked up startled and saw the moon shining clear in the heavens far above his head and at his feet a huge sea of mist. From a "deep and gloomy" opening in the vapor some distance from him, there mounted the sound "of waters, torrents, streams/Innumerable, roaring with one voice." In that deep thoroughfare, says Wordsworth, "Nature lodg'd/ The Soul, the Imagination of the whole."

Nature often works, Wordsworth tells us, upon the outward face of things as with imaginative power. Nature thrusts itself forth upon the senses; then imagination feeds upon the inner reality beyond it. Imagination molds, abstracts, and combines—"By sensible impressions not enthrall'd/ But quicken'd, rouz'd, and made thereby more fit/To hold communion with the invisible world." When the scene had passed away, it appeared to the poet "The perfect image of a mighty Mind,/Of one that feeds upon infinity." The single chasm through which the united sound of waters roared seemed analogous to the creative mind whence power arises from the dark abyss and takes shape in the world of light and form.

Wordsworth believed in an *anima mundi* operating in terms of benevolence and in some degree of purposiveness. But in *The Prelude* of 1805 he does not, as has been pointed out, portray external nature as without flaw or as universally benign to man. There are dark places and terror in the world around him and dark places in the mind. In childhood, when he stole the woodcock from another boy's trap, nature implanted in his mind "low breathings" coming after him. When he took the boat that belonged to another, "huge and mighty forms" moved slowly through his mind by day and were a trouble to his dreams. In young manhood, he woke in terror from the nightmare of the Arab carrying the stone and the shell to destruction. When he was in Paris soon after the September massacres, the fear gone by pressed on him almost like the fear to come. As he contemplated the outrage and bloody violence done in the name of liberty, ghastly visions of despair filled his dreams.

Yet, for Wordsworth, the bleakness and terror never exist for themselves alone; they potently serve that sense of religious sublimity with which imagination invests them. "A dark inscrutable workmanship" reconciles discordant elements and gives them directional force "to impregnate and to elevate the mind." Nature uses ignoble means for noble ends:

> How strange that all
> The terrors, pains, and early miseries,
> Regrets, vexations, lassitudes interfused
> Within my mind, should e'er have borne a part,
> And that a needful part, in making up
> The calm existence that is mine when I
> Am worthy of myself!
>
> (1850);1:344–50)

The imagination mysteriously selects and transforms the elements of fear as well as those of beauty that will administer to the strengthening of "the immortal spirit."

Wordsworth quite naturally assumed a dichotomy between conceptions of "beauty" and of "fear"—a dichotomy derived from a whole century of speculation on the beautiful and the sublime. These dual qualities were used not only to characterize the opposing poles of the external world but also to indicate the range of human emotion. Herbert Lindenberger calls attention to the rhetorical tradition, one with which Wordsworth was familiar, which distinguishes between *pathos,* the sublime in nature and the more violent emotions in man, and *ethos,* the beautiful in nature and those emotions in man which are calm and gentle. The progress from *pathos* to *ethos,* according to this scholar, "is Wordsworth's image of the history of his own life, and as such it provides a pattern of organization for *The Prelude.*"[7]

The first half of the poem moves from the awesome visionary experiences of childhood to the "tamer argument" of the human world of London; the second half advances from his experience of the terrors of the revolution, with the corresponding turmoil in his mind, to the attainment of inner peace. Until his residence in France in his late youth, man had been subordinate to nature, "His hour being not yet come," but Beaupuy converted him to the revolution and his allegiance was given to the people.

Still there is a stage beyond loyalty to the revolutionary cause. The revolution had been born of violence and had been carried forward on a wave of terror. Wordsworth, likewise, even to the very passing of his youth, had "too exclusively esteem'd *that* love,/And sought *that* beauty, which, as Milton sings,/Hath terror in it."

Hence, after his return to England, violent conflicting stresses over the revolution and the war with France led the poet to rationalism, and rationalism led to the impairment of the imagination and moral bankruptcy. But, as he approached maturity, nature bade him "seek for other agitations, or be calm," and Dorothy helped to soften down his "over-sternness." Finally *pathos* (violence) was controlled and directed to *ethos* (calmness and love). The poet intends the chastening process, described in book 13 (211–68), to mark his transition to manhood and his acceptance of a selfless or self-forgetting love. The attainment of "this love more intellectual" was a moral victory for Wordsworth and is the climax of *The Prelude*. Thus intellectual love is the second major theme of the poem, and it is closely intertwined with the account of the growth of imagination:[8]

> Imagination having been our theme
> So also hath that intellectual love,
> For they are in each, and cannot stand
> Dividually.
>   (13:185–88)

The person whose intellectual life has been grounded in imagination is *capable* of love, and he can be taught to love. As Wordsworth states it even more strongly: "This love more intellectual cannot be/Without Imagination."

An important supporting theme of *The Prelude* is the love of common man. This theme first makes its appearance in book 4 when, during a summer vacation at Hawkshead, Wordsworth viewed in a new perspective the goodness of the simple country people living there. He saw with another eye the quiet woodman in the woods, the shepherd on the hills, and even old Dame Tyson falling asleep over her Bible. His sympathies were also deeply stirred at that time by his encounter with the vagrant soldier whom he befriended and helped on his way. In book 7, which tells of his residence in London, he is witness to the pathos, the dignity, and the mystery of man in the great city, but somehow he seems isolated from the masses of mankind.

In book 8 he reviews the steps by which the love of nature led him to the love of mankind. The nobility of man, he reminds us, had early been impressed upon him as a boy through his admiration of the mountain shepherds. This idealization of individual shepherds and of the society of dalesmen in the Lake Country remained steadfast in his young manhood. These men of the pastoral community he consciously sets up in contrast to the brute masses of the city. In London he had felt intensely the "spiritual essence of Human nature" and the unity of man, but in the country his trust in "Man ennobled" was confirmed.

However, Wordsworth's trust had not been tested. For a long time following the "melancholy waste of hopes o'erthrown," when the French had turned a war of freedom into one of conquest, Wordsworth foundered desperately in search of steadfastness and knowledge. But at last the restoration of his creative imagination lifted his "Being into magnanimity," and nature deeply reestablished intellectual love. Thus revived, with a clearer sense of what was excellent and right, he came to see that ambition and folly impel the rulers of the world and that the wealth of nations is lodged in individual man alone. Thereafter, he set his course to seek in man as a person what there is of universal good.

As a result, he was especially anxious to learn the real worth and power of mind of those who lived by bodily labor. Eagerly he turned to the countryside and the public roads where he began to question those he met and to talk familiarly with them. There he saw into the depth of human souls and found in lowly men dignity, steadfastness, and honor. Wordsworth recognized that in rural communities excess of labor and poverty often thwart love; and love does not easily thrive in the cities. But in the country there are many living in the daily presence of nature who are rude in outward show, yet "men within themselves." He passionately declares that he will do justice in his verse to these simple men who too long have been neglected by snobbery:

> Of these, said I, shall be my Song; . . . my theme
> No other than the very heart of man
> As found among the best of those who live
> Not unexalted by religious faith,
> Nor uninformed by books, good books though few,
> In Nature's presence.
>
> (12:239–44)

The theme of common man is among the most exciting of the ideas that move through *The Prelude*. As the topic develops from book to book, the poet seems to glow with the sense of fresh discoveries. Best of all, he jubilantly realized that man as he idealized him in boyhood is still to be admired and is most worthy to be memorialized in his poetry.

Several topics that relate to the central themes of *The Prelude* are the ministry of books, the rejection of the "picturesque," and the poet's treatment of characters. In book 5, Wordsworth tells of what he "owed to books in early life." There is much uselessness, he says, in study and learning, especially of the sort pursued by a child prodigy in piling up rote knowledge under the strict guidance of a tutor. It would be better to have back again the old fairy tales and romances; better to let a boy roam wide in books of his own choosing than for him to be confined and protected. Tales of the marvelous, such as the *Arabian Nights,* that charm away the hours and keep alive the sense of wonder are especially to be prized.

"Untaught things, creative, and enduring" seemed to Wordsworth much more important than what was learned in schools. He insists on letting the child be himself, on letting him gain emotional stability through the rough and tumble of the school grounds. Let mankind have, he says, a race of rugged, natural children suffering and doing wrong, yet "in happiness/Not yielding to the happiest upon earth."

> May books and nature be their early joy!
> And knowledge, rightly honor'd with that name,
> Knowledge not purchas'd with the loss of power!
> (5:447–49)

The poet speaks with awe of the power in great books of science and poetry such as the Arab in the dream was bearing off. Wordsworth recounts the pleasures he received from reading words of poetry in tuneful order and from his discovery of "the great Nature that exists in works/Of mighty Poets." He finds visionary power embodied in the mystery of words. The right books rightly used, he concludes, are an aid to imagination and a support to the lessons learned from nature.

Soon after his return from France, Wordsworth tells us in book II his faculties fell under the dominance of the analytic intellect and remained so enthralled until his deliverance by his sister Dorothy. His response to nature was then contaminated; his mind was so far perverted that he began analyzing natural scenery in the fashion of picturesque—scene hunters like Gilpin and Price. He became obsessed by the habit of comparing scene with scene and of observing the "meagre novelties of colour and proportion." Wordsworth also says that at this time of intellectual thraldom the tyranny of the bodily eye drove him insatiably to seek "new forms,/New pleasure, wider empire for the sight."

His attitude toward nature then was identical to that which Wordsworth experienced on his first visit to Tintern Abbey when his passion for colors and forms was rapacious and when the hold of physical nature upon his eye was absolute. But the period of the eye's dominance (and the concomitant appeal of the pictorial and the picturesque in the landscape) did not last long. Through Dorothy's ministrations, Wordsworth escaped from the bondage under which he had fallen. He had felt too forcibly in early life the visitations of imaginative power for the imprisonment of his sight to last. In the course of time, the eye's eager delight was subdued by a mighty passion, and he stood again in nature's presence "a sensitive and creative soul."

All the characters in *The Prelude* are solitaries: the blind beggar, the "girl who bore a Pitcher on her head," the lone Arab on his dromedary, the vagrant soldier, the boy who blew mimic hootings to the owls. Even Wordsworth's intimates are viewed in isolation: Michel Beaupuy, Dorothy, Coleridge in Sicily as "lonely wanderer," and the poet's beloved schoolmaster, William Taylor. At the center of this world of solitary figures stands, of course, the most important solitary of them all—the poet himself. In the various confrontations between Wordsworth and his solitaries, he usually establishes a dramatic interaction that results in a revelation of some sort. His encounter with the blind man illustrates how he does this.

When Wordsworth was moving through the crowds in London's overflowing streets, he tells us in book 7, it seemed that everyone who passed him by was a mystery. All shapes appeared as in a dream, neither knowing him, nor known. But once, lost amid the shifting pageant, he chanced upon the sight of a blind beggar propped against the wall and wearing upon his shirt a written paper to explain his story. Confronted with that spectacle, his mind turned round "as with the might of waters": it seemed to him that in that label "was a type,/Or emblem, of the utmost that we know,/Both of ourselves and of the universe." In this dramatic meeting with the beggar, the poet kindled to an inward response. Out of what might have been a commonplace encounter came mystic communion and revelation.

Throughout *The Prelude*, Wordsworth casts himself in the reflector role. As he did in his chance meeting with the blind beggar, he surrounds his solitaries with a sense of mystery and then captures their mysteriousness as it rebounds to him. They are all, in one way or another, dramatic projections of the poet's self. Hence, each meeting with a solitary in its own special way advances the thematic development of *The Prelude*.[9]

Language, Structure, and Style

Wordsworth vowed, when nearing the completion of *The Prelude,* that if he could henceforth "write a narrative Poem of the Epic kind," he should then "consider the *task* of my life over." One knows from his own testimony that he undertook *The Prelude* because he did not feel ready for the epic task: "I was unprepared to treat any more arduous subject and diffident of my own powers."[10] But when he was well launched into *The Prelude* and the way seemed clear before him, he acknowledged the epic impulse behind the poem:

> O Heavens! how awful is the might of Souls,
> And what they do within themselves, while yet
> The yoke of earth is new to them, . . .
> This is, in truth, heroic argument.
>
> (3:178–82)

In the prospectus to *The Recluse,* Wordsworth had hailed Milton for justifying new areas worthier of epic treatment than wars of physical violence. Then, in his own poem of discovery, he went beyond Milton to find heroic argument in man's (indeed, in *one* man's) internal history. *The Prelude* developed into an epic of personal quest, a search of self-comprehension but at the same time it was to be universally representative. For, as Wordsworth says, "There's not a man/That lives who hath not known his godlike hours." The hero in *The Prelude* became Everyman in an epic search for "majestic sway."

Besides blazing a trail for new thematic conquests, Milton also gave to Wordsworth the will to create a fully worked-out poetic structure of epic scope. Ernest de Selincourt long ago took note of the epic structure of *The Prelude.*[11] The poem, de Selincourt observed, is not unlike an epic which, with its episodes, vicissitudes, and climax, goes a kind of circuit. The narrative begins at the end. The poet at the age of twenty-nine now "safe in haven relates the odyssey of his soul and imagination." The first eight books relate how nature quickened his sensibilities and molded his mind in childhood and youth, how he was consecrated to his great task, and how his powers progressed and expanded through early manhood. The ninth book reveals the poet at the height of a "buoyant but untried faith." The tenth book recounts the unsettling of his hopes, the distress of mind, and the moral skepticism he suffered. The last books tell of recovery from despair, of reconciliation, and of the restoration of creative imagination. The spiritual cycle at the close is completed, and the poet, like every epic hero, enters into his true heritage.

Through the years, Wordsworth made a number of changes in the structure of *The Prelude* that increased its overall strength. He enhanced the dramatic appeal by adding, subtracting, and moving about various pieces. Several of the best parts were first written and published as separate poems and later skillfully woven into the whole: for example, "There Was a Boy," "Simplon Pass," and "Influence of Natural Objects." The "spots of time" in Book 11, composed in 1798–99, were held back and used later as climactic examples of the power by which imagination is restored.

Wordsworth, in revising the 1805 version, removed portions that impeded the forward movement or seemed irrelevant to his purpose. The story of Vaudracour and Julia, which is the concealed story of his passion for Annette Vallon, was seen in perspective to be transient rather than permanent in the growth of the poetic mind. The lengthy tale of the shepherd's son, who went to rescue sheep and had himself to be rescued, was eliminated from book 8. Its excision strengthened the continuity of the structural contrasts between the paradisical country of Wordsworth's boyhood and the various literary paradises of the past. These paradises, in turn, were set free to draw upon the appeal of fairy stories and romances in an earlier book. Throughout *The Prelude,* Wordsworth establishes links of contrast and parallelism that unify the structure. To those already mentioned may be added, for illustration, the summer festival of Helvellyn, book 8, placed in opposition to London's Bartholomew Fair, book 7; and the return in book 10 of the poet to the shores near Furness Abbey.

Repetition is a settled principle of organization in *The Prelude.* Again and again Wordsworth tries to find new ways to invoke the inexpressible, to reveal eternity in its innumerable guises. Often his attempts repeat themselves in his meetings with the various solitaries. Sometimes they take the form of a struggle for definition in "the spots of time." As the poem advances, progress toward revelation is by no means in a straight line nor on a steady course. Perhaps, as Lindenberger suggests, the repetitive pattern should be regarded as one of alternation—between fealty to the demands of "inner" reality and eternity and to those of the "external" world. During his soul's odyssey the poet not infrequently discovers new ways of looking at things through a rebound from the negation of worldly experiences. The satiric episodes with their earthy bluntness especially serve to enhance the radiant, intuitive insights that precede or follow them.

Wordsworth was temperamentally adverse to satire, but he does use it effectively in *The Prelude* as a repetitive pattern of alternation. Satiric passages ("smudges of time") build up and set off passages of spiritual insight ("spots of time"). The satire comes chiefly in books 3, 5, and 7, on Cambridge, false learning, and the emptiness of city life. Also briefly in book 11 the "cult of the picturesque" is ridiculed. In book 3 Wordsworth protests compulsory chapel attendance and laments the shallowness of the college preachers:

> Our eyes are cross'd by Butterflies, our ears
> Hear chattering Popinjays; the inner heart
> Is trivial, and the impresses without
> Are of a gaudy region.
>
> (3:456–59)

He is critical of academic authority and especially of the grave elders, "Men unscour'd, grotesque in character." Cambridge was a kind of pageantry of the past world soon to be revealed to him in all its folly in London. The satire of book 5 is directed against the system of false learning propagated by the followers of Rousseau. They create the child prodigy, perfect in learning and in books, treading a path choked with grammars, but swollen with vanity and living "a life of lies." In the city of London Wordsworth finds foolishness scattered everywhere, but his scorn is most pointedly directed against the empty eloquence of a young politician "winding away his never-ending horn" and against the elegant, mincing ways of a worldly London preacher:

> There have I seen a comely Bachelor,
> Fresh from a toilette of two hours, ascend
> The Pulpit, with seraphic glance look up,
> And, in a tone elaborately low
> Beginning, lead his voice through many a maze,
> A minuet course, and winding up his mouth,
> From time to time into an orifice
> Most delicate, a lurking eyelet, small
> And only not invisible, again
> Open it out, diffusing thence a smile
> Of rapt irradiation exquisite.
>
> (7:545–56)

The sardonic language of this Miltonic parody—indeed, the drab descriptive language of most of book 7—is a far remove from the language of personal vision that precedes it in book 6 and that follows it in book 8. So, too, the other satiric books fall roughly into a pattern of repetitive alternation with what goes before and what follows. It is basic to the poem's design that imagination must first be impaired before its triumphant restoration at the end of the poem. The repetitive alternations in books 3 and 4, 5 and 6, 7, and 8 support in lesser contrapuntal waves this cyclic pattern. *The Prelude* would have been much flatter and impoverished if it had moved, as Wordsworth first planned it, directly from the adolescent exultations of book 4 to the triumph he celebrates in the final book.

The Prelude is not a miracle of architectonics, for Wordsworth did not plan it carefully in advance nor follow any one purpose throughout. The poem is the more convincing because of its spontaneity. Its truths are discovered by a great creative artist in the very process of surveying his past and with no thesis to prove. At the same time, the poet as craftsman has put together the pieces of his odyssey in such a way that the result is a unified poem of masterful construction and largeness of vision.

Much of the unity comes from the imagery of the poem. At first he reacted in a sensuous way to the physical world about him. As a child he

> . . . held unconscious intercourse
> With the eternal Beauty, drinking in
> A pure organic pleasure from the lines
> Of curling mist, or from the level plain
> Of waters colour'd by the steady clouds.
> (1:589–93)

From "pure organic pleasure"—"felt in the blood, and felt along the heart"—the poet passed through sweet purgations until his mind was shaped "to majesty" and consciously prepared for spiritual intercourse unprofaned by forms. This entrance into communion with "eternal Beauty" was the goal of his discursive mental explorations in *The Prelude*. Yet, in the midst of his journeyings to this visionary world, the poet had at all times a real solid world of images about him.[12] This world of forms and images— water, islands, mountains, breezes, and growing things—provides the basic setting for the poem. When Wordsworth describes a stream he knew in childhood, he can start out on the level of literal description; but before the reader has read much further the stream has become a metaphor for the workings of his imagination.

The dominating images of *The Prelude* are wind and water, images which by their very nature serve as intermediaries between the observable world and the higher, transcendental reality the poet wishes to make visible. In the opening of the poem the breath of the external wind and the inner breath of inspiration are brought together and connected with the creative process. By such mergings of the animate and inanimate worlds Wordsworth communicates in poetic terms the sense of the spiritual unity of all existence, a unity he had felt so overwhelmingly on an intuitive level in early childhood. And, by moving freely from the real to the visionary world and back again, he carries us with him in his adventure of discovery.

Some readers have felt that the language of *The Prelude* is overly abstract. Donald Davie in *Articulate Energy* (1955), however, has shown that Wordsworth's vocabulary is neither abstract nor concrete; it is something between the two.[13] Its verbs are concrete and pinpoint the main movements of Wordsworth's thought; the nouns and qualifying phrases recreate the full ebb and flow of the meditative process. Davie quotes and examines a key passage in book 2—the one in which the infant at his mother's breast rouses to an awareness of his existence—and shows how, in the 1805 version especially, Wordsworth conveys the power and the particularity of the situation by the precisely discriminated energies of his verbs. Two or three examples serve to illustrate the point: "the Babe,/ . . . Doth gather passion from his Mother's eye!"; "his mind spreads,/Tenacious of the forms which it receives"; "Along his infant veins are interfus'd/The gravitation and the filial bond/Of nature." In such a passage as the one analyzing the psychological stirrings of the babe, Wordsworth presents the meditating mind in all its fullness.

There is a great range and variety of style in *The Prelude*, as would be expected in so long a poem. Fluctuations in subject matter and mood call naturally for stylistic adaptations. For example, in book 3, college life at Cambridge is viewed critically, even satirically; and it is accordingly presented in a matter-of-fact, sinewy style. But, in book 4, in sharp contrast to the style in book 3, there is flowing, often eloquent poetry recounting the poet's suprapersonal communings with the living God. So, throughout the poem, the style adjusts amply and sensitively to the changes called for by the varied situations. There are few passages in *The Prelude* that are rough or flatulent: "My drift hath scarcely,/I fear, been obvious" (5:290–91). When necessary, Wordsworth knew how to take care of workaday details in a businesslike manner. The reader does not object to following the poet through the plains and foothills, for he knows that he will be led in time to the mountaintops.

Eminences in style emerge frequently; they do not usually continue for long stretches, but can be seen in passages of two to three dozen lines where the thought and imagery unfold harmoniously together. Readers of *The*

Prelude soon learn to identify and enjoy these select passages, such as those recounting the theft of the boat (1:401–27), the dedication to poetry (4:330–45), the boy on Winander (5:389–413), and Simplon Pass (6:556–72). Sometimes there are gemlike passages that fuse in two or three lines, as for example: "Bliss was it in that dawn to be alive,/But to be young was very heaven" (10:693–94). Sometimes memorable phrases occur in isolation, such as, "The noble Living and the noble Dead" (10:970).

Wordsworth was the master of all the rhetorical devices useful to the poet, but he did not make a display of them. To make the skating scene more vivid, he used onomatopoeia: "All shod with steel,/We hiss'd along the polish'd ice" (1:460–61). To mimic the shouting of the owls, he played upon enhancing vowel tones: "with quivering peals,/And long hallos, and screams, and echoes loud/Redoubled and redoubled; concourse wild/Of mirth and jocund din!" (5:401–4). He knew how to use rhetorical contrasts for emphasis: "I grew up/Foster'd alike by beauty and by fear" (1:305–6). Certain patterns of repetition he seems to have picked up from Milton. One of the best examples of Miltonic repetition for stress of thought and musical effect (which includes a triple repetition and a chiasmus) is the passage where sound is translated into vision:

> the soul
> Remembering how she felt, but what she felt
> Remembering not, retains an obscure sense
> Of possible sublimity, to which
> With growing faculties she doth aspire,
> With faculties still growing, feeling still
> That whatsoever point they gain, they still
> Have something to pursue.
> (2:334–41)

Wordsworth also learned from Milton the sonorous use of proper names, though he did not have the power to make names reverberate sublimely as did the author of *Paradise Lost*. Throughout *The Prelude,* there are Miltonic verbal echoes, but especially in those parts written in 1803 and after. Wordsworth borrows a phrase from *Paradise Lost,* for example, for the opening of his preamble, "The earth is all before me," (1:15), which is an echo of the closing lines of the expulsion of Adam and Eve: "The World was all before them where to choose." Another notable borrowing from Milton occurs in the last line of the great passage on Simplon Pass. The awesome features of the pass are transformed in the poet's imagination to types and symbols of eternity, "Of first and last, and midst, and without end," which is an appeal to Revelation 1:8 ("I am Alpha and Omega, the beginning and the ending, saith the Lord, which is, and which was, and which is to come, the Almighty") that is also paraphrased by *Paradise Lost,* 5:165: "Him first, him last, him midst, and without end." Examples of Miltonic influence can easily be multiplied, but their use should not be exaggerated.[14] Whatever Wordsworth used from other authors or from the tradition of rhetoric, he made his own.

As has already been indicated in passing, *The Prelude* published posthumously in 1850 differs in many respects from the poem read to Coleridge in 1806. Wordsworth made important revisions in 1828, 1832, and 1839, which altered the whole manner of the poem. The original was an intimate personal epistle addressed to Coleridge when the two were on terms of the closest intimacy. Wordsworth felt that before the poem could be given to the public, he would have to make it less personal. He also wanted to amend faults of ambiguity and loose expression. In revising, he succeeded to a considerable extent in making the language more controlled and exact and the meaning clearer. Some fine passages were written in the later years, such as the lines on Sir Isaac Newton (book 3). But many of the stylistic changes are injurious to the freshness, naturalness, and frankness of the early version. Revision often obscured a simple, naïve experience, or it replaced the living fact with an intellectual statement about it.

Revision also resulted in vital changes in thought as well as in expression. The early text of *The Prelude* gives us a Wordsworth who has a vibrant faith in "natural piety." But after the pressure of years and crushing personal sorrows, the poet Christianized his creed. As a consequence, the revised *Prelude* is overlaid with Christian thought. The original sections in which he exulted in the powers of his own mind, for example, are shorn of their daring and are deliberately expressed in less appropriate, more conventionally Christian terms. In the revision, Wordsworth also tones down his attack on Cambridge; and he presents France and the revolution with less glamour and with an increased conservatism. The later Wordsworth had forgotten much that the younger poet was trying to do in *The Prelude.* Consequently, his revisions were sometimes ruinous both to the honesty of the original and to its energy and freshness of style. Both versions of *The Prelude* are, of course, important, but the reader who wishes to capture the poet when he is most himself should concentrate on the 1805 version.

Chapter Five
Poems in Two Volumes, 1807

In 1807 Wordsworth gathered together and published a number of poems, enough to make up two volumes, written since the publication of *Lyrical Ballads* (1800). The new poems differ substantially both in subject matter and in style from those in *Lyrical Ballads*. Many poems were composed in a great outburst of poetic inspiration in the spring of 1802. They include sonnets in the Italian pattern, odes in both forms favored in the eighteenth century, and poems in a wide variety of meters, as well as "The Barberry Tree," discovered in 1964.[1] During his first year of residence in Grasmere in 1800 Wordsworth, who was inspired by imaginative sympathy for the shepherd folk in the Lake Country, immortalized the affections of pastoral life in "The Brothers" and "Michael." But by the end of 1800 the vein of pastoral poetry was spent, and Wordsworth needed time to work out new forms and to collect new experiences.

The year 1801 was one of comparative noncreativity; however, the poet was not idle. He undertook the modernization of three Chaucerian poems and thereby sharpened a facility in "rime royal" that was to benefit him in the composition of "Resolution and Independence." In 1802 he also found some promptings to his invention in the stanzaic patterns of Ben Jonson and Drayton. For his diction as well as his versification in the 1807 volumes he harked back to these and other favorite Elizabethan poets. From time to time he also adopted new stanzaic forms because of special associations. As a result, *Poems* of 1807 shows Wordsworth as experimenting in an extensive range of verse forms, often with spectacular success.

Of even greater significance than the advances of prosody in the new poetry is the shift in subject matter and mood. In *Lyrical Ballads* Wordsworth for the most part turned his back on his personal life, but in *Poems* of 1807 he found sources of inspiration in his own "heart-experience" and "soul-illumination." As in *Lyrical Ballads,* there are a number of narratives of human life in the 1807 volumes, but the stories are not bleak and naked; rather, they are rendered lyrically from the impulse of the poet's mood and reflect it. In *Lyrical Ballads* there is little politics, but *Poems* of 1807 contains a magnificent series of sonnets on public affairs.

Also, as Wordsworth settles into maturity in 1802, there is a movement toward greater concentration upon moral and spiritual problems. He becomes acutely aware of the fading of "the visionary gleam" and undertakes to answer the question "why" in the Immortality Ode. He begins to lose confidence in instinctive response to sustain his moral being and offers a mature adjustment in "Ode to Duty." Finally, when faced with the tragic loss of his brother John, he courageously submits, as he says in "Elegiac Stanzas," to a new control. In a number of significant ways, then, *Poems* of 1807, composed when Wordsworth was at the height of his powers, reveals an inward struggle from which emerged a man and a poet newly integrated.

Sonnets

Wordsworth told Landor that he once thought the sonnet an egregiously absurd form of composition. But one day in May 1802, when his sister Dorothy read aloud to him the sonnets of Milton, he was "singularly struck with the style of harmony, and the gravity, and republican austerity of those compositions." He took fire and produced three sonnets that same afternoon. The form proved to be congenial and in the years ahead he made extensive use of it. In all, he published over five hundred sonnets, covering a wide range of subjects in some of which can be found his best poetry. He was, moreover, the most prolific sonneteer in English.

One of the sonnets he composed that May afternoon was "I grieved for Buonaparte," the earliest of a flood tide of verse to be dedicated to national independence and liberty. Wordsworth was passionately alive at that time to the great drama of his country's struggle with France. During the brief interval of peace in 1802 he visited Annette and their child for a month at Calais. While there he wrote seven sonnets, only one of which was related to the reunion ("It is a beauteous evening calm and free"). This sonnet of spiritual amplitude and serenity he addresses to his daughter Caroline, "Dear child, dear girl," who bears within her the eternal presence of God.

The other sonnets all have to do with Wordsworth's zealous concern for European affairs and for England's part in them. Looking back from Calais at the "Fair Star of evening" stooping over England, he feels resurgent love for the country of his birth ("Composed by the Sea-side, near Calais, August, 1802"). All around him he discerns perpetual emptiness in the character and actions of the French people. But he is no less dismayed by the crowds of his own countrymen hastening to Paris to capture, if possible, a glimpse of Napoleon: "Ye men of prostrate mind, . . ./

Shame on you, feeble Heads, to slavery prone!" ("Calais, August, 1802"). Calais stirred vivid memories of his earlier visit to the city with Robert Jones in 1790 when French citizens were joyously celebrating the fall of the Bastille and "faith was pledged to new-born Liberty" ("Composed near Calais, August 7, 1802"). But in August 1802, when France proclaimed Napoleon first consul for life and decreed a state ceremonial in his honor, Wordsworth watched the people go indifferently about their tasks. To the poet, the contrast between then and now was agonizingly poignant ("Calais, August 15, 1802"). The promise of that "young dawn" had led to a dark noon presaging storm.

An ominous awareness of the great peril to liberty in England and Europe, which Napoleon's rise to power forewarned, was building up in Wordsworth. Liberty, which the young man had embraced, was now suddenly brought back into sharp focus. With militant energy Wordsworth released the fullness of his mind in stately and majestic regret over the loss of freedom for Venice, "eldest child of Liberty" ("On the Extinction of the Venetian Republic"). In the sonnet "To Toussaint L'Ouverture," he offered an emotional response to the heroic sacrifice of the Haitian leader who gave his life for freedom's sake. The poem closes with language that reverberates with the universal sharing of all creation in the cause of liberty.

Following the month's sojourn in Calais, Wordsworth returned to England, where he continued his exhortations in liberty's defense. London looked quite different to him from what it had one month before as he had passed over Westminster Bridge on his way to France. In the famous sonnet "On Westminster Bridge" the city is a sight "touching in its majesty" in which all objects, conditions, and moods conspire to bring nature and humanity into "an ennobling harmony." On his return to the city, he utters a cry of anguish over the worldliness of the present generation: "The homely beauty of the good old cause/Is gone." He calls upon Milton as the supreme example of moral virtue who in the stagnant present could lift men once again to "virtue, freedom, power":

> Milton! thou should be living at this hour:
> England hath need of thee: she is a fen
> Of stagnant waters: . . . We are selfish men;
> Oh! raise us up, return to us again;
> And give us manners, virtue, freedom, power.
> ("London, 1802")

In another sonnet, "Great Men Have Been among Us," he celebrates other English leaders of the Civil War—Algernon Sidney, Andrew Marvel, James Harrington, and Henry Vane the younger—but above them all towers the figure of Milton: "Thy soul was like a Star, and dwelt apart."

The notes sounded in the first London sonnets reverberate in those written when war with France was renewed in 1803 and through the entire series produced at intervals during the war. Prospects of invasion silenced Wordsworth's indignant rebukes and called forth what was heroic in his nature. "To the Men of Kent" is a spirited salute to the "Vanguards of Liberty" who did in times past win from the Normans "a gallant wreath." The crisis of Napoleon's victory at Jena in 1806, as empire after empire fell before the conqueror, roused an exultant battle cry of defiance: "And We are left, or shall be left, alone;/The last that dare to struggle with the Foe. . . ./O dastard whom such foretaste does not cheer!" ("November 1806"). During the war years Wordsworth's passion for liberty was tempered into a sinewy wisdom that also had something ennobling in it. Liberty, he declares, is not a free gift of nature, but must be won and maintained at the cost "of ceaseless effort, vigilance, and virtue." It is not achieved by military victory nor shaped by governors trained in battle; nor will the protective barrier of the Channel waters save it: "By the soul/Only the nations shall be great and free."

The great sonnet "The World Is Too Much with Us" has the same mood as those poems written in September 1802 that lament the unworthiness of the times—"Getting and spending, we lay waste our powers:/Little we see in Nature that is ours." The sonnet has a sea setting ("This sea that bares her bosom to the moon"), which may very well be a memory of Calais. In any event; it speaks with the same agitated passion that energizes the patriotic sonnets of 1802:

> For this, for everything, we are out of tune;
> It moves us not.—Great God! I'd rather be
> A Pagan suckled in a creed outworn;
> So might I, standing on this pleasant lea,
> Have glimpses that would make me less forlorn;
> Have sight of Proteus rising from the sea;
> Or hear old Triton blow his wreathèd horn.

Two splendid sea pictures are offered in sonnets about ships: "With Ships the Sea Was Sprinkled" and "Where Lies the Land to Which Yon Ship Must Go?" Three sonnets on sleep tell of agonized nights of sleeplessness, probably in the spring and summer of 1802, and of poignant supplications "To Sleep." One of these, which G. M. Harper calls "a perfect sonnet," opens with a series of beautiful images:

> A flock of sheep that leisurely pass by,
> One after one; the sound of rain, and bees
> Murmuring; the fall of rivers, winds and seas,
> Smooth fields, white sheets of water, and pure sky;
> I have thought of all by turns, and yet do lie
> Sleepless!

The diction is unpretending and the cumulative associations and rhythmic movement conducive to drowsiness. The rhyming, easy and natural, creates a relaxed response—"stealth," "wealth," "health." There is no need to know the reason for the poet's sleeplessness. The condition is common enough among all readers, as is the anguish in not being able, even with the most soothing incantations, to bring longed-for sleep.

Some critics of Wordsworth do not care for the patriotic sonnets. For example, John Jones finds that "the famous sonnets read like exercises, repellent often in their provincial self-importance" (*The Egotistical Sublime*); and F. R. Leavis sees the worst of the sonnets as "lamentable claptrap, and the best, even if they are distinguished declarations, are hardly distinguished poetry" (*Revaluation*). However, Middleton Murry thinks "the patriotic sonnets incomparably finer than any other poems in conscious praise of England," and a goodly company of reputable judges share this view.

The militant sonnets, whatever their worth as poems (and at least two of them rank very high—"To Toussaint L'Ouverture" and "London, 1802"), are important as a record of Wordsworth's advance from the poet of rapturous impulse to the poet of duty and fortitude. The emergence of Napoleon challenged Wordsworth's integrity and consummated the restoration of it. No poet of his temperament could pass through the tremendous experience of that struggle wholly unchanged. It quickened the stoic element in him and taught him to be less withdrawn in inspired contemplation and more concerned with the actual buffetings of life. It made him realize that acceptance of "the dreary intercourse of daily life," which in Tintern Abbey days seemed so repellent to him, comes close to being the whole wisdom of life. In any case, it was in this mood of acceptance of the real world in terms of daily living that Wordsworth married Mary Hutchinson on 4 October 1802. This event foreshadows the poet's submission to the control of "Duty" two years hence and a still more sobering acceptance of life in 1805 that was demanded of him by the death of his brother John.

"Resolution and Independence"

There are more of the essential features of Wordsworth's work in "Resolution and Independence" than in any other of the greater lyrics. Coleridge considered this fine poem especially characteristic of the author. It offers conflicting moods and responses: it ranges through joy and despondency, mystic insight and frugal moralizing, matter-of-factness in details of language, and glorification of the deepest passion. Dorothy records in her Journal (3 October 1800) the incident on which the poem was based: "We met an old man almost double. . . . He had had a wife, and she was 'a good woman, and it pleased God to bless us with ten children.' All these were dead but one, of whom he had not heard for many years. . . . He had been hurt in driving a cart, his leg broken, his body driven over, his skull fractured." "His trade was to gather leeches, but now leeches were scarce, and he had not the strength for it." Two years later, Wordsworth created a new account of the meeting with the old leech-gatherer to which he united more recent experiences and moods.

The poem opens on a glorious morning after a night of storm. The world is joyous and alive: the songs of birds make a sweet orchestration against a background of "pleasant noise of waters." Visual images in the second stanza further testify to the morning's radiance and epitomize nature's vitality in a single brilliant image:

> —on the moors
> The hare is running races in her mirth;
> And with her feet she from the plashy earth
> Raises a mist, that, glittering in the sun,
> Runs with her all the way, wherever she doth run.

Into this idyllic scene Wordsworth introduces himself not merely as an observer but as a fellow sharer with his whole heart. "I describe myself," Wordsworth wrote in a letter to Sara and Mary Hutchinson, "as having been exalted to the highest pitch of delight by the joyousness and beauty of nature."[2]

> I saw the hare that raced about with joy;
> I heard the woods and distant waters roar;
> Or heard them not, as happy as a boy.

Then, in a sudden inexplicable change of mood from joy that could "no further go," he is plunged to one of lowest dejection:

> And fears and fancies thick upon me came;
> Dim sadness—and blind thoughts, I knew not, nor could name.

His anxieties range wide; then he begins to particularize them. He has lived his whole life "As if life's business were a summer mood"; now visions of hostile days, of "Solitude, pain of heart, distress, and poverty," overwhelm him. His mind is filled with thoughts of the miserable reverses that have recently befallen young poets:

> I thought of Chatterton, the marvellous Boy,
> The sleepless Soul that perished in his pride;
> Of Him who walked in glory and in joy
> Following his plough, along the mountain-side;
> By our own spirits are we deified:
> We Poets in our youth begin in gladness;
> But thereof come in the end despondency and madness.

His brother poets, Thomas Chatterton and Robert Burns, had begun in gladness; but both had been cut down tragically in their youth. What happened to them (and what seemed to be happening to Coleridge) could easily happen to him. Wordsworth's health at that time aroused in him great anxieties. He suffered from prostrating headaches and from sleeplessness, and he had fears that his often exhausting travails of sustained creativity might have to be paid for in the end.[3] He sums up the young poet's curse in the profoundly oracular line: "By our own spirits are we deified."

From his fit of depression, which may have an element of the supernatural about it, he is rescued by what seems "almost an interposition of Providence." The lonely figure of the age-ravaged leech-gatherer appears as though miraculously summoned to confront the poet's ominous forebodings. Wordsworth drives home the helplessness of the old man: he is "the oldest man who ever wore gray hairs." Utterly alone, he is obviously unloved and uncared for; and his body is bent with infirmity. In a first draft the poet drew him with unsparing realism, likening him to the dead-alive figures in a cottage chimney corner: "He seem'd like one who little saw or heard/For chimney-nook or bed or coffin meet." In response to shrewd criticism from his sister-in-law, Sara Hutchinson, who failed to see the spirituality of the poem, Wordsworth cut out these lines and put in the famous protean similes of the stone and the sea beast, which serve as the imaginative core of the poem:

> As a huge stone is sometimes seen to lie
> Couched on the bald top of an eminence;
> Wonder to all who do the same espy,
> By what means it could thither come, and whence;
> So that it seems a thing endued with sense:
> Like a sea-beast crawled forth, that on a shelf
> Of rock or sand reposeth, there to sun itself;
>
> Such seemed this Man, not all alive nor dead,
> Nor all asleep—in his extreme old age.

In these and the following stanzas the old man is represented as at once real, almost grotesquely so, but at the same time he is an object of wonder and mystery. He has become merged with the landscape and associated with the primeval quality of life itself. He takes on a spiritual existence transcending the very processes of nature, a source of permanence amidst the flux. By a skillful handling of imagery, Wordsworth suggests a connection between the leech-gatherer and something that is majestic and permanent in nature: "Motionless as a cloud the old Man stood,/That heareth not the loud winds when they call;/And moveth all together, if it move at all."

The poet enters into conversation with him: "This morning gives us promise of a glorious day. . . . What occupation do you there pursue?" The old man answers, with feeble voice but with stately speech "such as grave livers do in Scotland use," that he came to the pond, old and poor as he was, to gather leeches—a hard and luckless trade by which, with God's help, he manages to make an honest living. Before the leech-gatherer finishes explaining his business to the poet, his words become muffled, and his figure fades into a dream landscape:

> The old Man still stood talking by my side;
> But now his voice to me was like a stream
> Scarce heard; nor word from word could I divide;
> And the whole body of the Man did not seem
> Like one whom I had met with in a dream;

> Or like a man from some far region sent,
> To give me human strength, by apt admonishment.

Wordsworth has almost fallen into a trance, just as he had when he met the blind beggar on the streets of London on whom he gazed "As if admonished from another world." However, he was not yet ready to accept the solution to his foolish anxieties that the old man's words provided. His former thoughts return:

> the fear that kills;
> And hope that is unwilling to be fed;
> Cold, pain, and labour and all fleshly ills;
> And mighty Poets in their misery dead.

Lewis Carroll and Edward Lear in their parodies have made capital of the irrelevance of Wordsworth's response to the leech-gatherer. But Wordsworth is so enmeshed in the imaginatively fatal sin of willful despair that it takes a prolonged impact to arouse and free him. A second moment of vision echoes and elongates the first:

> the lonely place,
> The old Man's shape, and speech—all troubled me:
> In my mind's eye I seemed to see him pace
> About the weary moors continually,
> Wandering about alone and silently.

Wordsworth finally realizes that in the old man there has been no decay of the inner life to correspond with that of his outer existence, and that despondency of spirit is not a necessary consequence of physical decline. When he understands the significance of the cheerful dignity of the decrepit old man, Wordsworth's tension is resolved, and he laughs himself to scorn. The last lines of the poem confirm in the simplest words—they are all that are needed—the truth of the experience for the poet: " 'God,' said I, 'be my help and stay secure;/I'll think of the Leech-gatherer on the lonely moor!' "

In few poems does Wordsworth achieve so great a perfection of form as he does in "Resolution and Independence." Though it contains striking contrasts in expression and style, they all move harmoniously toward the fulfillment of the poem's central purpose. The type of stanza used is ornate and very rare in Wordsworth's verse. Known as rhyme royal, it was picked up from his translations of Chaucer; it also derives from Chatterton's "Excelent

Balade of Charitie." The elaborate double simile is another instance of complexity and refinement of style. Yet "Resolution and Independence" is basically a poem of profound simplicity. The one central incident is outwardly the most ordinary sort of occurrence.

The figure of the lonely leech-gatherer is drab, to some readers even ludicrous. In an earlier version of the poem sent to Mary and Sara Hutchinson, Wordsworth included an account of the leech-gatherer's former life, his marriage, his ten children, and such matter-of-fact details as "He wore a cloak, the same as women wear . . ./And furthermore he had upon his back/Beneath his cloak, a round and bulky Pack." Wordsworth spiritedly defended these earthy details against the censures of Sara, who criticized them as "tedious," though amusingly enough he omitted some of them when the poem appeared in print. Even in its final form, however, there is an ample supply of prosaic features. These stand in startling contrast to the dignity and full musical resonance of the early stanzas with their Spenserian harmonies. Earthy detail and colloquial language were employed by Wordsworth not through any arbitrary whim, but because through them he could establish in universal terms the spiritual reality of the old man's existence. He could not have communicated in any other way a realization of "the native grandeur of the human soul" and its unconquerable fortitude.

Dove Cottage Lyrics and Memorials of a Tour in Scotland

Poems of 1807 contains nearly all of Wordsworth's best-known lyrics and his most charming poems of flowers, birds, and butterflies. Markedly different from most of the poems in *Lyrical Ballads,* they represent Wordsworth predominantly as a nature poet. In practically all of them the influence of Dorothy is striking and noticeable. As a child and as a young man Wordsworth preferred the austere beauty of the Lake Country and the Alps and had not paid much attention to the details of nature. Dorothy, on the other hand, was most remarkable for her powers of observation and for her overriding enthusiasm for the smaller details and the gentler aspects of nature. When the poet and his sister came to live together at Racedown, she infected her brother with her preferences and delights, an influence he gratefully acknowledges in *The Prelude.* She softened down, he says, his oversternness and planted the crevices with flowers.

For seven long years the joyous companionship begun at Racedown was uninterrupted, but in the spring of 1802 life at Grasmere was approaching an end. William and Dorothy were soon to leave Dove Cottage for some months to go to France and later to Yorkshire for William's marriage. The lyric entitled "A Farewell" (composed 29 May 1802), which apprehends the moment of their departure, is addressed in affectionate terms to the "sweet garden-cottage" in which the brother and sister had known near-perfect "soul companionship." The poem offers a loving tribute to William's bride as the new mistress of Dove Cottage, but it makes no attempt to hide the emotional crisis occasioned by the end of years of private intimacy between the brother and sister.

Other lyrics anticipating the coming change dwell with bittersweet poignancy on the poet's recollections of his childhood with Dorothy. An early member of the group is "The Sparrow's Nest." The chance discovery of a sparrow's nest in the shrubbery of the garden at Dove Cottage brought back "a vision of delight" of a similar nest in the hedge at their father's home which, as children, he and his sister had intently watched. Even then, "a little Prattler among men," Dorothy in visiting the sparrow's nest had those "humble cares and delicate fears" which in maturity continued to be a blessing to the poet. In another poem, "To a Butterfly," he recalls again how, even as a child, Dorothy set an example of tenderness.

There are also poems in which Wordsworth recounts their shared adult experiences; of these, the most famous is the poem on daffodils. This kind of poem he would not have written had he not learned to see through Dorothy's eyes. One windy day in April 1802, as the poet and his sister were passing through Gowbarrow Park along the shore of Lake Ullswater, they saw "a crowd,/A host of golden daffodils,/Fluttering and dancing in the breeze." In her journal passage on the daffodils Dorothy has made full use of her imagination in describing them. She endowed the daffodils with human attributes—"some rested their heads upon these stones as on a pillow for weariness; and the rest tossed and reeled and danced, and seemed as if they verily laughed with the wind." She likens the long belt of them along the shore to a busy highway of jostling people with "here and there a little knot, and a few stragglers" that in no way disturb the simplicity and unity of the show. In all of Dorothy's many recordings of the sights and sounds of nature, none surpasses the touch of creative magic she displays here.

When her brother set out to make a poem about their adventure, which wasn't until several years later (ca. 1804), he had his work cut out for him. What he does is to intensify the immediacy of the experience by confining it to his own person and to dramatize it by heightening the sense of sudden discovery. At the moment of revelation the wind was blowing over the lake directly on all that was before it, awakening both the waves and the crowd of daffodils into agitated motion. When Wordsworth recalled the original experience, perhaps through reading Dorothy's account of it, his tranquillity was disturbed by the awakening of the creative spirit, which, even as the wind gave life to external nature, gave to the "forms and images" living in his memory "a breath and everlasting motion." In the poem the wind's action draws all parts of the composition together and relates them to the whole. It is the breath which, in the climax of recollection, fills his heart with pleasure and sets it to dancing with the daffodils. Though the subject of the daffodil stanzas is, as Wordsworth reminds the reader in a note, rather an elementary, and primarily an ocular, impression, this lyric captures what must be a nearly universal response to natural beauty. For "I Wandered Lonely as a Cloud" is not only the most popular of all Wordsworth's lyrics; it is also the most frequently anthologized poem in the English language. And in the ending, which repeats a theme seen earlier in "Tintern Abbey," the poet tells us that the scene will provide future restoration.

The Dove Cottage poems, coming as they do midway between youth and middle age, alternate between the happy and the darker moods of the poet. Among the more joyous lyrics must be numbered "The Green Linnet," in which Wordsworth, from his sequestered orchard seat, greets "the happiest guest/In all this covert of the blest":

> Amid yon tuft of hazel trees,
> That twinkle in the gusty breeze,
> Behold him perched in ecstasies,
>   Yet seeming still to hover;
> There! where the flutter of his wings
> Upon his back and body flings
> Shadows and sunny glimmerings,
>   That cover him all over.

In this song of welcome to the linnet, the poet magically joins the art of great word painting to felicitous music that seemingly takes its very life and motion from the bird itself.

Free and cheerful, also, are the flower poems in which Wordsworth hails the small celandine, ill-requited "Herald of the Spring," and the daisy, "unassuming Common-place/Of Nature." In these poems Wordsworth elaborates on the idea that delight in the beauties of flowers is self-created—"my own delights I make"—and fancifully pursues with an easy, joyous inventiveness his responses to their habits and even moralizes upon them. Not all the flower poems, however, are lighthearted; at least one, "The Small Celandine" (composed in 1804), is as bleak as the early ballads. On a rough spring day the poet discovered an old celandine, "an altered form,/Now standing forth an offering to the blast,/And buffeted at will by rain and storm." Wordsworth's brooding mind wonders at the helplessness of the flower that in its youth had always been protectively responsive to sun and cold, "a flower of wiser wits." Now it "cannot help itself in its decay." In splenetic mood, the poet observes a close parallel between the flower's state and that of man. In the last stanza he draws the moral in what might have been a trite maneuver. But the encounter with the real flower is so genuinely an encounter of a middle-aged man threatened by his own helplessness that meaning and symbol are joined with absolute naturalness.

Paralleling to some extent the austere thought evoked by the lesser celandine are the famous lines on "Yew-Trees." All his life Wordsworth was enthralled by the beauty, majesty, and antiquity of living trees, but nowhere is his response to trees more magnificently expressed than in this poem. He begins by describing the solitary yew of Lorton Vale "of vast circumference and gloom profound," of form and aspect too magnificent ever to be destroyed. But of still worthier note are the fraternal Four of Borrowdale. With figured verse and with a more artful diction than he customarily uses, the poet majestically summons up the awesome spirit of primeval mysteries in the umbrageous presence of these huge trees. In *Modern Painters* Ruskin calls "Yew-Trees" "the most vigorous and solemn bit of forest landscape ever painted." Wordsworth himself placed it among his category, Poems of Imagination.

The more sonorous temper of "Yew-Trees" is also found in "The Affliction of Margaret," written in 1804 perhaps originally for inclusion in a new edition of *Lyrical Ballads*. It is a heartrending poem on the maternal grief of "a poor widow of Penrith." "She kept a shop," says Wordsworth, "and when she saw a stranger passing by, she was in the habit of going out into the street to enquire of him after her son." Her pathetic plea is cast in majestic phrase and rhythm that differ from Wordsworth's earlier ballads:

> Perhaps some dungeon hears thee groan,
> Maimed, mangled by inhuman men;
> Or thou upon a desert thrown
> Inheritest the lion's den;
> Or hast been summoned to the deep,
> Thou, thou and all thy mates, to keep
> An incommunicable sleep.

But this brief survey of the Dove Cottage poems may be concluded on a happier note with a few comments about one of Wordsworth's most delightful pieces: "Stanzas written in my Pocket-copy of Thomson's *Castle of Indolence*." In Spenserian stanzas, a form he rarely used, Wordsworth describes himself and Coleridge during their joyous companionship in the early Grasmere days. The first four stanzas describe Wordsworth and the next three Coleridge, each a happy spirit indulging himself in his own eccentric behavior. With fine imaginative insight Wordsworth shares with the reader the intriguing vagaries of the genius of himself and his friend and the intense reality of their happiness.

In August 1803 William and Dorothy set off with Coleridge on a tour of Scotland, but, because of ill-health, Coleridge separated from his companions at Loch Lomond. The Wordsworths continued on by themselves, visiting the Highlands and stopping over for a week with Sir Walter Scott at Lasswade. Their six weeks' journeying brought them into contact with a mass of new impressions, which Dorothy recorded in *Recollections of a Tour Made in Scotland*. What the two travelers sought most of all was an emotional involvement in landscape to which a human figure was linked. Just such a scene unfolded before them when they came suddenly at dusk upon a lonely Highland boy calling the cattle home for the night: ·

His appearance was in the highest degree moving to the imagination: mists were on the hillsides, darkness shutting in upon the huge avenue of mountains, torrents roaring, no house in sight to which the child might belong; his dress, cry, and appearance all different from anything we had been accustomed to. It was a text, as Wm. has since observed to me, containing in itself the whole history of the Highlander's life—his melancholy, his simplicity, his poverty, his superstition, and above all, that visionariness which results from, a communion with the unworldliness of nature.[4]

For Wordsworth the supreme gift of the tour was precisely such moments of visionariness that fed his imagination and became transformed in due course into poetry. He made no poem upon the Highland lad in his isolation; he chose instead the lonely Highland girl working and singing by herself as she harvested the grain.

During their tour Wordsworth and his sister would have seen women reaping the grain and timing the strokes of the sickle to the harvest song. Upon his return home he composed "The Solitary Reaper" after reading the following sentence in Thomas Wilkinson's *Tour in Scotland*: "Passed a female who was reaping alone: she sung in Erse, as she bended over her sickle;

the sweetest voice I ever heard: her strains were tenderly melancholy, and felt delicious long after they were heard no more." Wilkinson's words tersely and admirably establish the facts of the poem, but Wordsworth's trenchant imaginative recollection vitalizes the loneliness, melancholy, simplicity, and, most of all, the mysteriousness associated in his mind with the people of the Highlands. He underscores the reaper's isolation by repeating four times over in the first stanza that she is a single human figure in the landscape.

The aloneness of the singer is further intensified in the second stanza when she is compared to the lone nightingale singing in far-off Arabia and to the solitary cuckoo "Breaking the silence of the seas/Among the farthest Hebrides." The melancholy tone and rhythm established in the first stanza are developed in the third stanza. Mysteriousness is achieved by means of the reaper's song. The spectator cannot understand her foreign tongue; hence, the theme of her "melancholy strain" is shrouded in mystery. The poet, in contemplating the possible theme of the song, pushes back the boundaries of time and space. The theme, whatever it is, could be past, present, or future; it could be some personal domestic sorrow or some universal loss; it could be near at hand, at home, or distant. The mystery of her plaintive song in that remote place becomes interpenetrated in the reader's consciousness with the mystery of all human experience outside the limit of time and space. Wordsworth not only captures the whole history of the Highlander's life; he isolates for one brief moment the mystery of sorrowing humanity in the melancholy song of the reaper. He reaches the farthest limits of imaginative awareness; yet the girl remains steadfastly the simple Highland lass cutting and binding the grain and singing at her work.

Another fine poem that closely and imaginatively involves a human figure with the landscape is "To a Highland Girl." Wordsworth says that his sister described "this delightful creature and her demeanor particularly" in her journal. In the poem she becomes the unifying center of a conflux of romantic recollections, enlivened by merriment, mellowed by kindness, but made unforgettable and radiant through beauty. The poet has no more claim upon the Highland girl as a person than upon "a wave of the wild sea." Imaginative re-creation transforms the memory of her to visionary loveliness, "heavenly bright," such as one might envisage in a dream. Yet she also belongs, "in the light of common day," to the scene of gray rocks, household lawn, half-veiling trees, waterfall, silent bay, and the quiet road by the cabin. Like the skylark, she is "true to the kindred points of heaven and of home."[5]

The poem that probably best expresses the spirit of the Scottish tour is "Stepping Westward." The courteous greeting of "two well-dressed women"

along the shore of Loch Katrine—"What, you are stepping westward?"—
wrought an enchantment upon the poet that opened up the spiritual meaning of his wanderings. The greeting was made "in one of the loneliest parts
of that region" and seemed a sound "without place or bound," a token
opening into infinity. It told the travelers, though they were traveling as
"guests of chance," that their stepping westward was "A kind of *heavenly*
destiny"; that, in the journey ahead, they had a "spiritual right/To travel
through that region bright." With this transcendental vision evoked by the
friendly greeting of the Highlanders there mingled also "a human sweetness" that would accompany the travelers on their endless way.

   One of the finest lyrics of the tour, "Yarrow Unvisited," resulted from
Wordsworth's contact with Scott and the balladry of Scott's countryside. It
is a kind of "recollection" in reverse; for, though William and Dorothy have
not been to Yarrow, William jauntily refuses to indulge his sister's wish to
go there: "We have a vision of our own;/Ah! why should we undo it?"—
presenting the paradox that the experience of a place seen only in the imagination is better than one seen with the eyes. The meter is the same as that in
"Leader Haughs," a poem by the "Minstrel" Burn, one of the last true wandering minstrels of the Border. Other ballads also contributed to "Yarrow
Unvisited," particularly the exquisite ballad of Hamilton beginning "Busk
ye, busk ye, my bonny bonny Bride/Busk ye, busk ye, my winsome Mar-
row!" By drawing upon real balladry and adding playful touches of dialect,
Wordsworth created in "Yarrow Unvisited" a truly delightful piece of Border minstrelsy.

"Ode: Intimations of Immortality from Recollections of Early Childhood"

   Wordsworth's great "Ode on Immortality" is not easy to follow nor
wholly clear. A basic difficulty of interpretation centers upon what the poet
means by "immortality." T. M. Raysor offers an impressive array of evidence
for believing that Wordsworth "was thinking of an individual immortality
which even took the form of resurrection of the body."[6] But Alan Grob,
who finds that Mr. Raysor draws his evidence substantially from the years
after the ode was written, sees nothing in works prior to 1804 implying any
conviction of hopes beyond the grave.[7] The majority of scholars believe,
along with Grob, that the term "immortality" in this poem does not mean
the endlessness of life; instead, it means the infiniteness of human consciousness.[8] The poet's primary task is the search for identity, whereby the

natural man can apprehend a continuous unity of consciousness, resting upon the abiding presence of a "spirit-life" through all phases of his life. The Ode had its origins in a serious crisis. In mid-March 1802 Wordsworth was visited by Coleridge, who complained despairingly of a loss of his creative powers. Induced by his mood, Wordsworth also became fearful that his own imaginative vision might be failing him. One week after Coleridge's departure and in answer to his challenge to the doctrine of hope, Wordsworth within five days composed "To the Cuckoo," "My Heart Leaps Up," and the opening strophes of the Immortality Ode. On 23 March Dorothy entered in her journal: "a mild morning, Wm. worked at *The Cuckoo* poem." The recollection of the cuckoo's voice on that day—it was not physically heard, for the first cuckoo did not arrive until the first of May that year—called into consciousness those "visionary hours" when the earth was apprehended with "bliss ineffable" and the poet saw in all things "one life and felt that it was joy."

It was a short leap to the Rainbow poem, composed on 26 March, in which Wordsworth reasserts his faith in the ongoing beauty and joyousness of existence. Wordsworth did not see the rainbow at the time of the poem's composition any more than he had heard the bird's voice when he wrote the poem on the cuckoo; he is probably recalling a rainbow he had seen in boyhood on a day of wild storm in the vale of Coniston.[9] But, through imaginative recollection, Wordsworth found himself transported, as he had during the composition of the cuckoo poem, to another sphere of being—to one more real than that of the senses. When he had such ecstatic experiences, he felt that he had passed outside time into eternity. In the Rainbow poem he poignantly expresses the hope that the rapturously beautiful sights of nature that in childhood opened to him another world through vision would continue to do so as long as he lived.

The next day, 27 March, "a divine morning, at breakfast, Wm. wrote part of an Ode." Now he confronts directly the fact that, with the passing of the years, the glory that had transfigured all things for him in boyhood had faded and he no longer sees things "apparelled in celestial light" except when meditation on the cuckoo's cry or recollection of the rainbow's splendor brought him once again to that world of vision:

> There was a time when meadow, grove, and stream,
> The earth, and every common sight,
>   To me did seem
>   Apparelled in celestial light,
> The glory and the freshness of a dream.

> It is not now as it hath been of yore;—
>   Turn wheresoe'er I may
>   By night or day,
> The things which I have seen I now can see no more.

So he states the irrevocable separation from past splendors and wrestles with
the problem of his loss through the next three strophes. In the second strophe the poet declares that all the lovely objects of nature are lovely still, but
in their presence he has changed: for him the glory is gone. In the third strophe, he forces a vigorous response to the joyousness of all creatures around
him on that glad May morning:

> Now, while the birds thus sing a joyous song,
>   And while the young lambs bound
>   As to the tabor's sound,
> To me alone there came a thought of grief:
> A timely utterance gave that thought relief,
>   And I again am strong.

The "timely utterance" was most likely the Rainbow poem written just the
day before the Immortality Ode was begun and expressing the conviction
that the paradisiacal vision of his childhood has been recovered and will survive in the future. So the response becomes affirmative: "The cataracts blow
their trumpets from the steep;/No more shall grief of mine the season
wrong." The cataracts, echoes, winds, and the shouts of the shepherd boy
have a mnemonic effect that causes the poet to participate in the holiday
spirit of renewal. But the affirmative movement is of short duration. For, although Wordsworth enters sympathetically into the joyousness of nature,
still for him a particular kind of vision was withheld:

> —But there's a Tree, of many, one,
> A single Field which I have looked upon,
> Both of them speak of something that is gone:
>   The Pansy at my feet
>   Doth the same tale repeat:
> Whither is fled the visionary gleam?
> Where is it now, the glory and the dream?

So the fourth strophe ends on a discordant note expressing a heavy sense of
loss and an implicit demand for an explanation of the cause of it.

In strophes 5–8 Wordsworth projects an explanation for his loss of vision that is based on the doctrine of preexistence—one probably suggested to him by Coleridge.[10] Both poets had realized the profound significance of childhood in the growth to mature manhood. In considering the recovery of his imagination as recounted in *The Prelude,* Wordsworth places great emphasis on the part played by the restorative power of imaginative moments recollected from his own childhood:

> O! mystery of man, from what a depth
> Proceed thy honors. I am lost, but see
> In simple childhood something of the base
> On which thy greatness stands.
>
> (*Prelude,* 12:272–75)

Now a reading of Plato and the Neoplatonists suggested that the dreamlike moments experienced in childhood were simply carryovers from the spirit realm from which the soul descended. Gradually, as the natural child grew up and forgetfulness set in, the celestial brightness dimmed and finally completely faded away. The universal myth of preexistence, though alien to Wordsworth's mind and connected to no other of his writings, was simply used by the poet as an account of his experience. When Wordsworth was criticized for teaching the strange doctrines of preexistence, he defended himself in a fine metaphor: "Archimedes said that he could move the world if he had a point whereon to rest his machine. . . . I took hold of the notion of pre-existence as having sufficient foundation in humanity for authorizing me to make for my purpose the best use of it I could as a poet." So Wordsworth put into the single, consistent myth of pre-existence experiences that were universal and that had happened to him but that remained untranslatable except in mythical terms.

As an example of his use of the myth, Wordsworth sets up Coleridge's small son Hartley, the "six years' Darling of a pigmy size," as a living example of the child possessed of power and domination. What is imperial about the child of the Ode is his visionary power that makes it possible for him to move into another world. He becomes "a mind/That feeds upon infinity"; though "deaf and silent," he reads "the eternal deep." Over him, "Immortality Broods like the Day." The child, of course, in time will grow up and lose his regal powers. Indeed, he bends all his efforts toward growing up, "at strife" with his own blessedness. Hence, the poet asks him wonderingly, "Why with such earnest pains doth thou provoke/The years to bring the inevitable yoke?" And he forlornly concludes: "Full soon thy Soul shall have her earthly freight,/And custom lie upon thee with a weight,/Heavy as frost and deep almost as life!"

In contemplating the fate of the child, the poet finds himself confronted by an impasse. The problem of the loss of ecstatic vision, he discovers, cannot be resolved through the presumptive evidence of preexistence. For the logic of preexistence led Wordsworth to the inescapable conclusion that maturity is a time of inevitable darkness and grief—a conclusion that ran counter to his own experience and to human experience in its totality. When he resumed the composition of the poem two years later, Wordsworth was on firmer ground.[11]

In the concluding strophes of the Ode, the poet is now convinced that the visionary splendor glimpsed in childhood is gone past recall; but he is equally certain that the indestructible elements that generate youth's vision persist in all stages of man's development. These "first affections," whatever they may be, are yet the "fountain light of all our day." Having once been, they still must be; and man can in thought revive them and be grateful for them. The ecstatic contemplation of nature is past, but now in its place the philosophic mind reads the "music of humanity" interfused everywhere in the visible scene. Thus the child is indeed father of the man. Childhood has the vision and manhood the wisdom, and their days are bound to one another by a continuous, indestructible spiritual energy. So the poet finds strength not only in the "primal sympathy" that by "invisible links" allies nature to the affections, but also in "soothing thoughts that spring/Out of human suffering." The child knows the natural world, but man has come to know the human world as well.

The controlling theme of the Ode is, therefore, identical with that of *The Prelude:* both poems trace the growth of the human heart. In childhood, imagination opens up the glory and the infinitude of nature; in manhood, nature inspires human affections that will bring strength and comfort. Hence, the poet still responds joyously to "Fountains, Meadows, Hills, and Groves." He has relinquished but "one delight" (the old visionary power) to live beneath nature's more habitual sway (the companionship that keeps "watch o'er man's mortality"). As he wished it in the Rainbow poem, the poet's days are joined "each to each by natural piety." At the poem's close, the world of nature becomes wedded to the world of man. All existence becomes significant and precious for its human-heartedness:

Thanks to the human heart by which we live,
Thanks to its tenderness, its joys, and fears,

> To me the meanest flower that blows can give
> Thoughts that do often lie too deep for tears.

Some critics have found weaknesses in the Ode. Coleridge heads the list with his complaint that the lines addressing the child as "Thou best Philosopher" is an instance of mental bombast—"thoughts and images too great for the subject." Frederick A. Pottle finds the poem marred by disparate ideas; other readers are troubled by what seem to be inflated thoughts and forced piety.[12] However, the majority of competent judges acclaim the "Ode on Immortality" as Wordsworth's most splendid poem. In no other poem are poetic conditions so perfectly fulfilled. There is the right subject, the right imagery to express it, and the right meter and language for both. Wordsworth happily chose the form of ode as best suited to the majestic subject with which he deals. The form was suggested by a disputation he and Coleridge had over the odes of Ben Jonson and by Coleridge's own use of the form. Wordsworth had never previously used such a meter, but in his poem it moves along with freedom and majestic dignity as though it came, in Keats's phrase, "as naturally as leaves to a tree."

The stately metrical form is matched by a simple but majestic structure: the three parts turn upon a crisis, an explanation, and a consolation. Some critics of the Ode complain of the abrupt transitions in the poem, particularly of the prolonged break occasioned by the preexistence theme. But one must not be disturbed or misled by the inclusion of this section. Besides the superb poetry of the fifth strophe, for which every lover of poetry is grateful, the Platonic middle section gives a shuttlelike movement and largeness to the Ode. Wordsworth uses this section to set off the lamentations of the first part against the exultations of the third and, as a great lever, to lift his theme. The concluding section rises to a moral grandeur that would have been impossible without the strophes on preexistence.

The language of the Ode is stately; the imagery is fresh. Images of light recur throughout the poem to give coherence and splendor to the theme. Also a humbler imagery emerges from time to time: that of the flower, the natural symbol of the beauties of nature which are the "breath of God," which threads its way through the poem until it reaches the climax of meaning in "the meanest flower that blows." The primary symbol in the poem is, of course, the child whose presence is continuous. Enough has been said already about the child's symbolic significance—enough, indeed, about the range of meaning and value given by a variety of readers to this amazing lyric.

"Ode to Duty," "Elegiac Stanzas," and "Character of the Happy Warrior"

"Ode to Duty," composed early in 1804, had its origins in conversations with Coleridge, who was conducting an investigation with himself on the nature and dislike of doing one's duty.[13] The poem ties in with the heroical last strophes of the "Ode on Immortality." In the "Ode to Duty," as with the more famous ode, the poet accepts the law of life fulfilled in terms of human love and self-sacrifice as a welcome replacement for the rapturous visions and unchartered freedom of his youth. Two types of characters are described in the poem as fulfilling duty's ordinance. First there are those (stanzas 2 and 3) who instinctively, with glad innocence, do duty's work and know it not:

> [Those] who, in love and truth,
> Where no misgiving is, rely
> Upon the genial sense of youth:
> Glad Hearts! without reproach or blot;
> Who do thy work, and know it not.[14]

Second (stanzas 4 and 5), there are those who, by transcending self, knowingly and willingly, submit to duty as objective law. In this class Wordworth places himself, not through any catastrophe or "strong compunction," but because, as he confesses, he has too long relied on his own freedom of choice and seeks the "repose" to be found in external control:

> Me this unchartered freedom tires;
> I feel the weight of chance desires:
> My hopes no more must change their name,
> I long for a repose that ever is the same.

Duty is invoked as the law of the universe. Nature takes a prominent place in the scheme of existence; but now the supreme power that moves the sun and the other stars is identified with the moral law: "Thou dost preserve the stars from wrong;/And the most ancient heavens, through/Thee, are fresh and strong." The bond to nature acquires a new name, and Wordsworth sets himself in a new relationship to it.

In a stanza included in the 1807 edition but subsequently omitted, Wordsworth described a third situation, an ideal as yet unattained in this world, in which human desire and self-interest spontaneously coincide with duty so that moral victory is always enhanced by enjoyment:

> Yet not the less would I throughout
> Still act according to the voice
> Of my own wish; and feel past doubt
> That my submissiveness was choice:
> Not seeking in the school of pride
> For "precepts over dignified,"
> Denial and restraint I prize
> No farther than they breed a second Will more wise.

In this statement of the ideal of duty, according to Newton P. Stallknecht, Wordsworth is following Schiller's doctrine of the *schöne Seele,* a subtle restatement of Kant. In Schiller's eyes, there is something beautiful about a character whose desires and interests have grown to coincide with duty itself. Hence Wordsworth, following Schiller, is advocating not blind submission to duty but free, eager acceptance of a moral law that cannot be interpreted as satisfying one's immediate desires. Although Wordsworth never reprinted the stanza quoted, Stallknecht sees the spirit of Schiller's "beautiful soul" reflected in the entire ode. Thus in man's imperfect world, persons of the second class, which includes the poet, win peace of mind by a self-imposed inner control and by happy acceptance of the guidance of a higher power. The "Ode to Duty" contains a dignified self-renunciation and a movingly honest confrontation to the law of life.

On 6 February 1805 Captain John Wordsworth of the merchant service went down with his ship off Portsmouth. He was the best-loved of William's brothers, "a Poet in everything but words," and his loss was an intense shock. For two months after John's death William wrote nothing at all, but by May he was able to finish *The Prelude.* However, it was the next year before he felt equal to the task of memorializing his brother in verse. He did so in "Elegiac Stanzas suggested by a Picture of Peele Castle in a Storm." The Picture was by Sir George Beaumont, and Wordsworth saw it in his patron's home during a visit to London in 1806. The poem was written soon afterward.

The tragic drowning of his brother confirmed the predominant soberness of life expressed in the closing stanzas of the "Ode on Immortality" and the "Ode to Duty." This devastating experience brought the poet's earlier and later moods into actual and acute antagonism. In "Elegiac Stanzas" the contrast between his present and former self are set forth in the pictorial symbol of Peele Castle. The poem opens with the recollection of a pleasant summer month spent on the coast with a view of the castle twelve years before. At that time the sea remained serenely calm day after day and the air still:

> How perfect was the calm! it seemed no sleep;
> No mood, which reason takes away, or brings:
> I could have fancied that the mighty Deep
> Was even the gentlest of all gentle Things.

If then, Wordsworth says, his had been the painter's hand to express what he saw, he would have added "the gleam,/The light that never was, on sea or land,/The consecration, and the Poet's dream." But this remoteness in his soul the poet rejects as illusory; in its place he accepts the consequences of human tragedy:

> So once it would have been,—'tis so no more;
> I have submitted to a new control:
> A power is gone, which nothing can restore;
> A deep distress hath humanised my Soul.

Beaumont's picture of the castle in the raging storm now seems a truer representation of life than the placid scene Wordsworth viewed as a young man. The storm with "the lightning, the fierce wind, and trampling waves" all remind him of the dreadful night in which John lost his life. No longer can he "behold a smiling sea" and be what he has been:

> Farewell, farewell the heart that lives alone,
> Housed in a dream, at distance from the Kind!
> Such happiness, wherever it be known,
> Is to be pitied; for 'tis surely blind.
>
> But welcome fortitude, and patient cheer,
> And frequent sights of what is to be borne!
> Such sights, or worse, as are before me here.—
> Not without hope we suffer and we mourn.

Two years before in the Immortality Ode Wordsworth took comfort in the enduring love of nature, which survived the loss of vision. But now life is no longer a chronicle of heaven; like the castle, life braves the ravaging storm. One does not have "soothing thoughts that spring/Out of human suffering"; instead, one has "fortitude, and patient cheer." With John's death, Wordsworth is forever separated from the unique spiritual joy he knew in youth. He accepts his loss and welcomes fortitude, which makes that and all other loss to come endurable. The last line of the poem suggests to some readers the Christian consolation of life after death. However one may choose to read that line, it is a fact that hereafter Wordsworth, who had earlier said "we find our happiness [here] or not at all" (*Prelude*, 10:728), turned toward the solace of traditional Christianity.

A second poem honoring his brother, "The Character of the Happy Warrior," also confirms the poet's new stoic attitude. The tragic death in the autumn of 1805 of Lord Nelson, whose heroic person the nation idolized, was the occasion for the lines. But Wordsworth himself said it was John's character that largely inspired them. The poem is by no means simply a eulogy of military life; the Happy Warrior is a heroic person in any walk of life who lives in obedience to an "inner light" or indwelling law. What guides him is the same power that "preserves the stars from wrong." He is a kind of personified ideal of the "Ode to Duty."

With the momentous group of poems written in 1804—"Ode on Immortality," "Ode to Duty," "Elegiac Stanzas," and "The Happy Warrior"—a great turning point in Wordsworth's thought is marked as he passed from a period of sheer self-dependence to one of vigorous stoicism and traditional Christian faith in his later life. In any case, it is ironic that as Wordsworth began to withdraw, to be less open to experience, he wrote some of his most moving poetry. The newfound austerity appears also in "The Song at the Feast of Brougham Castle" and in "The White Doe of Rylstone," stories of heroic martyrdom composed in 1807. In these poems, as in the great odes and the elegiac verses to his brother, fortitude and love, when put to the test in adversity, are transmuted to wisdom, even to beatification.

Chapter Six
The Excursion and After

Somewhere between 1805 and 1807 Wordsworth's poetic vitality began slowly to decline. With the fading of inspiration he thirsted for peace of mind—a desire that drove him gradually to adopt more conventional sentiments, attitudes, and forms. After years of self-questing and challenge, he no longer sought primarily to reform the reading public but more often to remind his readers of what they already knew and accepted. His poetical method, tone, and style also changed considerably. These alterations in thought and expression are reflected in *The Excursion,* written between 1803 and 1814.

The evolution of Wordsworth's opinions in this and later works was both honest and intelligible. He was not, as some have charged, "a renegade" to his faith, nor were his human sympathies contracted. Moreover, even as inspiration declined, Wordsworth's prosodic skills and technique continued to develop; much of the later poetry is, therefore, of high artistic craftsmanship. Foremost among the achievements of the later period is the revision of *The Prelude,* undertaken over the years, in which the poet created new beauties and at the same time often clarified and strengthened his poetry.[1] Other outstanding pieces of the later years include "Laodamia," "After-Thought," "Mutability," and "Surprised by Joy." The last-named, written 1813–14, has been called "the most poignant sonnet in the English language."

The Excursion

Wordsworth thought that *The Excursion* was the crowning expression of his genius, but not many critics have been very happy about it. Jeffrey's "This will never do!" sounded the battle cry of contemporary opposition that was echoed by Hazlitt and others and later confirmed by Matthew Arnold. In his essay on Wordsworth (1888), Arnold agreed that *The Excursion* could "never be to the disinterested lover of poetry a satisfactory work." Yet many of Wordsworth's contemporaries rated the poem highly. To Charles Lamb, it was "the noblest conversational poem I have ever read"; and Keats acclaimed it as one of the "three things to rejoice at in this age." It went through seven editions in the poet's lifetime and helped immeasurably to build up his reputation. However, soon after Wordsworth's death, *The Excursion* fell into almost total neglect from which it has not yet recovered. *The Prelude* has rightfully replaced *The Excursion* in critical esteem. Nevertheless, in spite of its failure to measure up to the lofty aspirations of the Prospectus, *The Excursion* remains an important work in the Wordsworth canon.

The "argument" of *The Excursion* is the vindication of man's right to hope by overcoming despondency and reestablishing genuine knowledge. In book 1, the theme of optimism is introduced by "The Ruined Cottage," a tragic story but one that suggests consoling thoughts. It is told to the Poet by the Wanderer, the prime sponsor of hope, whose own life history, to give authenticity to his views, is graphically set before us. The theme is expanded in books 2, 3, and 4 by the introduction of the rebellious, disillusioned Solitary, who impugns the cause of hope. Book 4, the heart of the poem, contains the bulk of the Wanderer's exhortations to the Solitary to correct his despondency. In book 5, the Pastor, who is introduced, supports the cause of hope with a series of stories (books 5–7) about those who lie buried in the churchyard. Finally, in books 8 and 9 the Wanderer applies the theme to a criticism of the social conditions of England.

As first conceived by Wordsworth and Coleridge while in the Quantock Hills, *The Excursion* was to be completely original.[2] Coleridge had predicted that his friend would achieve immortality with his "Recluse" as the first and finest philosophical poem, and Wordsworth himself in the highly original Prospectus seemed on the way to fulfillment of his friend's prediction. But when he came to write *The Excursion* (identified by Wordsworth as "the second part of a long and laborious work to consist of three parts and to be called *The Recluse*") his inspiration flagged. Instead of initiating a new genre, he fell back upon a kind of didactic poetry of retirement that was common in the eighteenth century, and was represented by such works as Edward Young's *Night Thoughts,* Mark Akenside's *The Pleasures of Imagination,* and William Cowper's *The Task.* To this dominant type in blank verse, Wordsworth merged the poetry of philosophical dialogue, of which the most notable example is John Thelwall's *The Peripatetic;* illustrative tales of humble life found in such poems as Shenstone's "School-mistress" and especially Crabbe's "Parish Register"; and meditations on life and death derived from the then-popular funeral elegies.

There was some originality in Wordsworth's synthesis of traditional materials, but on the whole it must be admitted, *The Excursion* has a disappointing air of archaism. The poem's greatest novelty, and to many its most attractive feature, is its setting in the Lake Country. The scenery described, though not recorded in detail, resembles the region of Furness Fells, except for the scene of Margaret's story in book 1, which is a village common in Somersetshire or Dorsetshire. Book 2 takes the reader to the cottage of the Solitary, situated on the high ridge between the Great and Little Langdales, and there the crucial debate of book 4 is held. With the introduction in book 5 of the Pastor, the scene shifts to the village of Grasmere. All in all, the natural surroundings make a marked contribution to the poem, especially to the opening and close.

Each of the major characters in *The Excursion,* as all critics since Hazlitt have realized, is a personified aspect of Wordsworth himself. The Solitary is professedly drawn from a certain Joseph Fawcett, "a preacher at a dissenting meeting-house at the Old Jewry in London." But his characterization is, in fact, largely taken from Wordsworth as he later interpreted himself during his contact with the French Revolution and his subsequent disillusionment over its failure. The story of the Solitary's suffering resulting from the deaths of a daughter and a son followed by the death of his wife closely parallels Wordsworth's loss of two of his own children in 1812, a short time before *The Excursion* was completed. Something of the authentic Wordsworth also comes through in the Solitary's response to mountain glory. When the storms ride high, he has heard the mysterious music the mountains give forth to Wordsworth's ear. The Solitary, too, like the poet on Snowdon, has had his rapturous vision on the mountain. But, unlike Wordsworth, the Solitary has not mastered his bitterness: he remains cynical, apathetic, and arrogant. He is what Wordsworth might have become if Dorothy and Coleridge had not rescued him.

The Wanderer, the leading character of *The Excursion,* is a detached spectator of rural life. He was brought up under the threefold influence of nature, strict family tradition, and the reverential worship of God. His boyhood and youth and that of Wordsworth, as set forth in the early books of *The Prelude,* are nearly identical. The original of the Wanderer was a "packman" Wordsworth had known during his schooldays in Hawkshead. He admired the occupation and defended the suitability of such a character to take a prominent role in *The Excursion.* Wordsworth said the Wanderer "represented an idea of what I fancied my own character might have become in his circumstances."

In the first book the Wanderer's character opens up a new perspective for the poet; unfortunately, as the poem progresses, he becomes at times unattractively self-righteous. The Pastor is hardly more than a narrator of other people's lives, though it is obvious that Wordsworth admires him and partly shares his views. Wordsworth brings the poet in as the spokesman for the whole. Thus the reader sees that each of the main characters bears resemblances to Wordsworth himself. The whole poem is, indeed, but a thinly veiled account of how Wordsworth over the years achieved a victorious adjustment to a series of crippling blows to his own hopes.

The action of *The Excursion* is spread over five summer days and includes only four main characters. As a story involving these characters it has little to recommend it, though some of the stories they tell have high merit. The vital center of interest is the doctrinal plot. This center is firmly established in book 1 with the biographical account of the Wanderer and with the story of "The Ruined Cottage." Through the ministry of nature and ardent thought the Wanderer had attained to hope and wisdom: "Unoccupied by sorrow of its own,/His heart lay open; . . . he could *afford* to suffer/With those whom he saw suffer." His heart grieved for Margaret whose tragic story he tells to show that it is possible, by means of active faith in divine wisdom, to convert earthly sorrows into positive good.[3]

In book 2 the reader becomes acquainted with the Solitary, who is introduced first through the eyes of the Wanderer so that the reader can get a proper perspective on the Solitary's errors and frailties. He is a sick man and not a philosopher; his illness consists of uncontrolled vacillations between excesses of self-complacency and personal grief, of apathy and zealous revolutionary ardor, of voluptuous immortality and cynical misanthropy. The discovery of his copy of *Candide*—"this dull product of a scoffer's pen"— reveals to the Wanderer how impoverished and prideful the Solitary had become. When the Solitary makes an appearance, one discovers that he still possesses true sensibilities: he greets the Wanderer with "an amicable smile" and comforts a weeping child; he responds to the wild beauty of the mountains. But his utter lack of faith is confirmed by the story he tells of the poor old pensioner driven to his death by the heartless indifference of a housewife. Even when the Solitary descends the mountain after finding the old man, the vision of a "mighty city" wrought by the great clouds piling up after the storm can have no meaning for him. He wants to believe, but he cannot.

At the opening of book 3, the mountain setting is read symbolically. The Wanderer sees in nature's forms "a semblance strange of power intelligent." But the Solitary can see the varied shapes before them only as "the sport of Nature." He regards the botanist or geologist who never bothers about the riddle of existence as happier than the Wanderer; and happiest of all is the thoughtless cottage boy. For the Solitary, death is "a better state than waking." As support for his despondency, the Solitary relates the story of his shattered life. His vain, self-indulgent youth was altered with marriage to a lovely bride. Two children were born to them, and they lived in undisturbed wedded happiness for seven years. Then abruptly both children died; soon after, his grief-stricken wife followed them, leaving him "on this earth disconsolate." Life became for him empty and meaningless.

From his dejection he was roused by the shock of the storming of the Bastille, and he becomes a convert to the French Revolution. But, when the French nation turned aggressor and when the zealots in England abandoned liberty's cause, the Solitary decided to leave his own country and to seek in America the "archetype of human greatness." But he soon became disillusioned with democracy in America and with "Primeval Nature's child," the Indian, who proved to be "A creature, squalid, vengeful, and impure." From his futile quest he returned to a sequestered existence in the Lake Country whence he looks apathetically upon the stream of life encompassed by evil; he cherishes no hope but that his "particular current soon will reach/The unfathomable gulf, where all is still!"

In book 4, the Wanderer, who steadfastly confronts the difficulties raised by the story of the Solitary, offers a way for him to overcome his despondency. The Wanderer opens his discourse by accepting the basic assumption of the Solitary that there is unavoidable suffering and evil in the world. But "the calamities of mortal life" may be offset by faith in a benevolent, superintending providence "Whose everlasting purposes embrace/All accidents, converting them to good." A trust in this infinite benevolent power is inspired by the beauty of the natural world and is supported by the enduring strength of moral law. Duty, aspiration, and hope exist outside the exigencies of change and are eternal. Thus, the Solitary has no right to despair because the glowing visions of his youth have faded.

The Wanderer, too, once experienced "fervent raptures" that are now gone forever, but he does not merely sink into apathy because of his loss. Moreover, the Wanderer has also shared the Solitary's faith in "social man." If the Wanderer shares it no longer, it is not because his hope for humanity has flagged but because he realizes that it takes time for mankind to be redeemed. The revolutionists have forgotten that man's nature cannot be changed in a day; man must learn "that unless above himself he can/Erect himself, how poor a thing is Man!" The Wanderer urges the Solitary to live a normal country life, to revisit the scenes of his youth, and (in a very Wordsworthian formula) to revive early memories, "the hiding places of man's power." For, as Wordsworth also tells us in *The Prelude*, "Strength attends us if but once we have been strong." One should rejoice in nature and, if tired with systematic thinking, let the fancy lead to superstition's airy dreams. Even superstition opens up a sort of truth that is better than doubt and despair.

In a famous passage, which enchanted the author of *Endymion*, the Wanderer tells how the enlightened Greek shepherd or hunter created divine forms from the living presence of nature. He counsels the Solitary to throw aside cynical Voltaire and to drink deep at the fountain of living experience and reality as did the Greeks. The Wanderer's argument culminates in a passage of remarkable beauty (4:1058–77). The soul, he says, has power to transmute all negative elements of its experience into new sources of strength. Despondency is corrected by "the mind's *excursive* power," the power of moving outward toward nature. And he concludes: "So, build we up the Being that we are;/Thus deeply drinking-in the soul of things,/We shall be wise perforce."

With the opening of book 5, the group leaves the mountain solitude, descends into the valley, and arrives at the village church. The Solitary reopens the problem of the predominance of evil by attacking baptism as an empty pretense and by reiterating his charge that the value of life declines from youth to age. The Pastor, who joins the disputants, gives his support to the Wanderer's optimistic faith in a benevolent providence. He asserts that solace for the calamities of life may be in part achieved by him "who can best subject/The will to reason's law," but that human reason alone has limitations. An inward faith is also required, one supported by active energy, tenderness of heart, and dignity of soul. In answer to the Solitary's request that he supply specific examples from life in place of abstract assertions, the Pastor offers the story of the sequestered quarryman and his wife as proof that happiness and virtue can exist in spite of arduous poverty. The Solitary objects that theirs is the exception rather than the rule and cites as more typical the case of the old pensioner.

In books 6 and 7, the Pastor tells a series of tales about the tenants of the churchyard to show, in a variety of ways, how some persons overcome their sorrow or suffering and some do not. The stories, offered as "solid facts" from real life, support the wisdom of reasonable optimism. Wordsworth lets the stories speak for themselves, though the intended moral is not far to seek. The Pastor, encouraged by the Poet, agrees to limit his narratives chiefly to those that excite feelings of the higher ethical sort: love, esteem, and admiration. However, he does feel that tales of evil sometimes should be told as a challenge to virtue.

Book 6 opens with the story of the rejected lover who achieved a victory by giving himself to science and "Nature's care" (an illustration of the means of restoration recommended to the Solitary in book 4). This story is followed by the account of the persevering miner who is redeemed, like one of Browning's characters, by his strength of purpose. Exactly opposite is the tale of the prodigal son, who in weakness followed dissolute ways in the city but returned repentent to his parents' door. The harmonizing influence of solitude is illustrated by the story of the Jacobite and the Hanoverian, who, though dire enemies in the world, found peace and affection in constant fellowship during their retirement. Much can be learned, the Pastor reminds his listeners, "in the perverseness of a selfish course," as exemplified in the story of the proud and despotic mother. After a prolonged resistance to benign influences, the mother achieves peace when she realizes the transience of her devotion to worldly passions.

In contrast to the tale of the avaricious matron, there follows the tragic and deeply moving story of Ellen. She is deserted by her lover and suffers other humiliations after the birth of her child, but in the end she is purified and ennobled by an edifying submission to divine will. At the insistence of the Wanderer, the Pastor relates the story of Wilfrid Armathwaite, a shepherd who seduced his own maidservant. Unable to find forgiveness in himself or to bear the weight of his shame, he took his own life. The gloom of this tale is relieved by the charming picture, which closes book 6, of the widower who finds consolation for his lost wife in the affection and joy that survive in his six daughters.

In one of the best-told stories of the series, a tale that opens book 7, a pampered, worldly clergyman is forced to take a modest curacy among the mountains. By accepting his lot and by faithfully performing his narrow duties, he finds spiritual equanimity. There follows a pair of stories about men with bodily afflictions who create full lives for themselves. The deaf man cultivates the grace of "pure contentedness" and becomes a source of hope to others. The blind man triumphs over his defect by actively engaging his remaining senses to enrich his mind until it is truly enlightened.

The series of stories closes with two tales that link Grasmere with the wider world. The first of these is about a heroic youth who leads forth a troop of volunteers from the peaceful valley during the alarm over Napoleon's threatened invasion. Death came at home to the youth from a moment's rashness, and he was buried with "a soldier's honours." The second of the tales is a kind of epitaph on a knight of Elizabeth's time, Sir Alfred Irthing, who fulfilled his vow "to redress wrong." The stories of the mountain youth and the knight emphasize the transience of human glory; the restless generations go to their decay while "the vast Frame/Of social nature changes evermore." At the end of book 7, the Wanderer courteously thanks the Pastor for all the stories he has told and asserts that they may be

accepted as "words of heartfelt truth" tending to teach patience under affliction, faith, hope, love, and reverence. By their example, the Solitary is offered the means of restoring his sense of "belonging" to life and his ultimate
regeneration.

In the final section, books 8 and 9, the Wanderer appraises the contemporary state of English society as it has been affected by the Industrial Revolution. He sees towns burgeoning, "barren wilderness erased," Britain's
ships peopling the high seas, and a mighty navy defending the blessed isle
"of Liberty and Peace." He exults in the mastery "of the forces of Nature" to
serve his will. But he is alarmed at the heavy price paid for material progress
by injury to the health of workers and corruption of the "old domestic mor-
als of the land." He sees families broken up by factory labor and children
enslaved to weakness and stupidity. The Solitary pointedly asks if there
haven't always been and if there aren't now tens of thousands of children
living in the country who are denied "liberty of mind" by abject poverty and
unremitting toil. This challenging question leads the Wanderer to the cli-
matic response that opens book 9: " 'To every Form of being is assigned'/
Thus calmly spoke the venerable Sage,/'An *active* Principle.' "

The "active Principle" pervades the universe; its noblest seat is the human
mind. In response to this power, man is free "to obey the law of life, and
hope, and action." Even old age is not separated from "the stir of hopeful
nature." But human injustice has brought about inequalities that obstruct
the operation of the active principle. To achieve "liberty of mind" for all
classes, the Wanderer calls upon England to "complete her glorious destiny"
by providing universal education. There is a famous passage that begins: "O
for the coming of that glorious time/When . . . this imperial Realm,/
While she exacts allegiance, shall admit/An obligation, on her part, to
teach/Them who are born to serve her and obey; . . ." (293 ff.). The passage is hardly great poetry, but it is an intellectually courageous utterance
and constitutes the climax on the constructive side of the argument of *The
Excursion*. It is a link to the earlier poetry mainly addressed to the correction
of despondency, and it reaffirms the liberty of mind founded on virtue. At
the close of the poem, the Solitary has not been restored to hope, but
Wordsworth seems to have planned to present his rehabilitation in some future work. In any case, the Solitary's recovery is not vital to the thematic
structure.

Wordsworth's primary purpose in *The Excursion* is to expound a "philosophy," though not in any sense formally to announce a system. Basic to his
teaching is the constantly recurring theme that nature is permeated with an
active intelligence that is universal and the source of all men's highest

thoughts and feelings. This active soul of nature spreads beyond itself communicating good. Any man who has lost hope may be restored to virtue by opening his mind to universal truths that are innate, immutable, and transcendental. In the process of recovering, however, human reason alone is not enough because it is liable to error. The entire story of the Solitary is, in fact, an example of the abuse of rationalistic thinking. The Wanderer says that the wildest superstitions are preferable to pure reason. Reasoning is an invaluable secondary power, but self-knowledge must be guided and enlightened by imagination. Since the source of enlightenment is nature, the Wanderer calls upon the Solitary to correct his irregular habits of living by communicating with nature with the full power of the *excursive* mind. By following this course, he will apprehend eternal moral truths, gain self-control and self-respect, and be reawakened to love for his fellow men. The path of duty that the Wanderer exhorts the Solitary to follow is not, in any strict sense, Christian duty. The concept of duty, like hope, is basically utilitarian. In establishing his philosophic position, Wordsworth makes slight use of the language of Christian doctrine. He skillfully and unobtrusively fuses naturalistic belief with tradition. Even the Pastor generalizes about his faith and shows at times a bias for Neoplatonic natural piety. Nevertheless, *The Excursion* does teach Christian faith and virtue and, in many respects, is more specifically religious than any of Wordsworth's previous works.

The Excursion cannot be considered an altogether satisfactory poem. As a whole, it lacks dramatic and narrative vigor. The reader is confronted by that "species of ventriloquism," of which Coleridge complains, "where two are represented as talking, while in truth one man only speaks." A common criticism is that Wordsworth has dealt unfairly with the Solitary by making him a man of straw. In answering the Solitary's arguments, the Wanderer is at times dogmatic and pietistic. However, Wordsworth does not intend for the two adversaries to meet on equal terms. The Solitary is a "sick" man and needs help. This help the Wanderer magnanimously offers even though it may at times seem to be given in a patronizing manner.

In the matter of style, it must be admitted that there is a decline from Wordsworth's best. There is an abundance of conscious artifice, inflated rhetoric, and prolixity. The use of personification has increased, imagery is frequently decorative and ornamental, and there is an inflated use of awkward words ("disencumbering") and of negative adjectives ("unambitious," "unsubstantialized"). Words of Latin derivation predominate over those of Anglo-Saxon origin; the double negative (always a favorite device of Wordsworth) is much too common; and there is too frequent use of parenthesis. In the narratives employed to correct despondency, Wordsworth is apt to force his points at the expense of the stories.

But *The Excursion* cannot be dismissed as the tiresome, inflated preaching of an aging poet. The central character, the Wanderer, has many qualities to recommend him. Though his role as peddler was ridiculed by Jeffrey, the choice was a characteristic and right decision for Wordsworth. The Wanderer represents the successful embodiment of the poet's unifying impulse of philosophy. He is the chosen vehicle to transmit the spiritual and infinite as an active force for truth, goodness, and love. The stories told by the Pastor offer a remarkable range of character types handled by Wordsworth with knowledge and power. Many of them were the life stories of Grasmere people personally known to the poet. These characters of the real world were individualized by the author with numerous vivid details and unique characteristics.

Though the style of *The Excursion* has its shortcomings, as has been indicated, it still contains, in the words of a recent scholar, "much wisdom, much beauty, and very little that does not in some way bear the stamp of a great mind."[4] There are many lovely images and individual noteworthy passages, such as that on the shell held to the ear of the child (book 4), the passage praising natural but mute poets (book 1), the picture of the moon (book 4), the Wanderer's youthful transports (book 1), the Solitary's speech on the twin peaks of Langdale and his account of the ending of the storm and his mystical vision (book 3), the child's imaginative flight initiated by listening to the minstrels (book 7), the Solitary's account of love (book 3), and the famous chronicle of the origin of the Greek shepherd's religion (book 4). Wordsworth's power to describe landscape remained "unimpaired and often strangely moving." This talent he reveals in countless small, deft strokes and in elaborate sketches like that of the white ram who is reflected in the still lake in book 9.

In spite of shortcomings, *The Excursion* is a significant document of Wordsworth's mind in a transitional phase before it has settled into conservatism. The poem has splendid bursts of eloquence, bold arguments lighted with felicities of phrase, fresh depictions of natural scenery, and courageous expositions of social philosophy.

The White Doe of Rylstone

The White Doe of Rylstone, begun in October 1807 and finished in January 1808, was not published until 1815, one year after *The Excursion.* Although *The White Doe* was composed earlier and is touched with the

ethereal magic of Wordsworth's earlier poetry, like *The Excursion* it deals
with the problem of human suffering. Moreover, in both poems the problem derives from the poet's confrontation of "keen heart-anguish" in his
own life. In *The Excursion,* as has already been pointed out, the response of
the Solitary to the deaths of his two children and of his wife closely parallels
Wordsworth's heartbreak over the loss of his own two children. Similarly,
Emily's lonely conquest of sorrow in *The White Doe* matches the poet's victory over numbing grief after the death of his brother John. Because of
Wordsworth's intimate, personal involvement with suffering, the poem is in
many ways his profoundest exercise of the spirit. As recorded in conversation with Justice Coleridge, Wordsworth himself believed it to be "in conception the highest work he had ever produced."[5]

For his story Wordsworth combined history with legend: the rising of
the northern earls during the reign of Queen Elizabeth I (as told in
Thomas Percy's *Reliques*) with the weekly visit of a white doe at Bolton
Priory (as set forth in T. D. Whitaker's *History and Antiquities of the
Deanery of Craven*). To these two elements, fused by poetic imagination,
he added a third agent, missing from the original action: Emily, daughter
of the Nortons. Richard Norton, father of nine sons and a daughter,
joined the rebellious earls in support of the Catholic religion, but
Wordsworth skillfully hints that some of the rebels were motivated by
conditions other than religious ones. Norton's motives, however, are sincere; and the poet treats him sympathetically. No attempt is made in the
poem to give a true or rounded account of the rebellion. There is no mention, for example, of Mary Queen of Scots though in history she was a
prime mover in the quarrel.

Wordsworth also leaves out the maneuvers and retreat of the earls and
concentrates on the Nortons alone in their glory and misery. The intricacies
of history have given way to the simplicity of poetry. There is no avoidance
of moving action, only a rigorous selection of it focusing upon the martyrdom of Emily. For the spiritualized conception of Emily's character, as
Wordsworth acknowledges in the dedication to Mary, the "celestial" Una of
Spenser's *Faerie Queene* served him as a glorious example. "The gentle Una
. . . pierced by sorrow's thrilling dart,/Did meekly bear the pang un-
merited." So Emily was singled out in *The White Doe* to endure the cruel
hammer blows of fate and to achieve a spiritual triumph over "pain and
grief."

The first canto is set in a period after the death of Emily, in order to create in the mind of the reader an aura of expectation and to establish what
Wordsworth calls "the shadowy influence of the Doe." "Soft and silent as a

dream," she comes each Sunday morning to the churchyard of "Bolton's moulding priory," where, during divine service, she quietly lies beside a grassy grave. She emerges as a creature with supernatural overtones and implicitly as a creature which, in Wordsworth's language, "by connection with Emily is raised as it were from its mere animal nature into something mysterious and saint-like." The Doe's kinship with Emily is anticipated by the creature's reclining beside a grave that was "the favoured haunt of Emily in her last years." The Doe's spiritual affinity is "Presumptive evidence" of involvement with a higher being, for, by the formula explained in a passage from Bacon's *Of Atheism* that is prefixed to the poem, beasts are ennobled by dependence on man, just as man is made noble by the protection and favor of God. The Doe, then, is established in the first canto as the emblem of Emily's spiritualization. The remainder of the poem is an "explanation" of the transfiguration of Emily and the Doe.

The second canto opens bleakly with the introduction of the "solitary Maid" whose only companion is "her sylvan Friend" and who exists in "a dearth/Of love upon a hopeless earth." The cause of her woes is a banner of war which, at her father's command, she embroidered with the sacred cross and wounds of Christ. The banner symbolizes the tragic action with which Emily and others had become involved. For Emily, it is a sign of impending disaster; for her father, a symbol of martial courage in a righteous cause; for the poet and reader, an emblem of Emily's patience.[6]

When the call came for Norton to join the rebels, he was confronted by a divided family. His eldest son, Francis, pleads with him not to go to war. But Norton, with "a look of holy pride," seizes the banner, thrusts it into another's hands, and leads forth eight sons to battle. Left behind in scorn, Francis grapples with his heart, is cleansed of despair, and envisages massive suffering but one not futilely negative. He decides to join his brothers unarmed, though he utterly forswears his father's course. When he sees Emily left alone, innocent of any offense to God or man, he counsels patience, and at first she does not understand. She realizes well enough that the action of her father will bring suffering; but she must learn, as Francis explains, that suffering requires action to master it:

> depend
> Upon no help of outward friend;
> Espouse thy doom at once, and cleave
> To fortitude without reprieve.

Emily cannot see what she is to become. Her temptation, as Francis foresaw, is still to hope for the safety of her family or for some change in the fortune of war.

But, in the next three cantos, Emily's patience emerges. She suppresses her desire to intercede in her father's doings. She knows that her duty is not to interfere in the course of events, but "in resignation to abide/The shock and finally secure/O'er pain and grief a triumph pure." Emily carries Wordsworth's meaning for what suffering holds of "permanent, obscure, and dark," but which also partakes of infinity. The *conquest* of her sorrows is the crucial *action* of the poem.

After the father and brothers are led off to execution, the survival of Francis provides a ray of hope. Emily is encouraged by the report that her brother has recovered the banner. Just as she had earlier resisted the attention of the Doe, so she now withdraws from the total acceptance of her doom. She still cannot realize the magnitude of her afflictions, but not for long. The sixth canto recounts the capture and death of Francis. On another level, it describes "the hammering of the final nail in the crucifixion of Emily" when she throws herself upon her brother's grave and is overwhelmed with "the whole ruth/And sorrow of the final truth!"

As the burial of Francis is the consummation of Emily's earthly sorrow, so the final canto is the consummation of her "anticipated beatification" through the "apotheosis" of the Doe. At the end of long wanderings in grief and trouble, Emily returns to Rylstone. She is forlorn, but her soul stands fast, sustained by memory and reason, and "held above/The infirmities of mortal love;/Undaunted, lofty, calm, and stable,/And awfully impenetrable." With the return of the Doe, Emily is cheered and fortified; she is able to revive the memories of the past, "undisturbed and undistrest." Natural haunts calm and cheer her; when the church bells sound their Sabbath music—"God us ayde"—her heart joins them in prayer. On favored nights she often goes to Bolton to look upon St. Mary's shrine and the grave of Francis; there she sits "forlorn, but not disconsolate." When she returns from the abyss of thought, she does not mourn but rejoices in life. Her sanction, however, is *inward* and stands apart from human cares; hence, she can proffer affection only to a creature of celestial significance—to the radiant Doe whose presence pervades the poem like a spirit, suggesting the mystic beauty of another world. The Doe shadows forth the joyful serenity that Emily's tortured spirit finally achieves. Wordsworth makes clear Emily's accomplishment and her relationship to the Doe in a letter to Coleridge in 1808:

[Emily] is intended to be honoured and loved for what she *endures,* and the manner in which she endures it; accomplishing a conquest over her own sorrows (which is the true subject of the Poem) by means, partly, of the native strength of her character, and partly by the persons and things with whom and which she is connected; and finally after having exhibited the "fortitude of patience and heroic martyrdom," ascending to pure, ethereal spirituality, and forwarded in that ascent of love by communion with a creature not of her own species, but spotless, beautiful, innocent, and loving in that temper of earthly love to which she alone can conform.[7]

In the closing lines the poet announces the culmination of Emily's triumph:

> From fair to fairer; day by day
> A more divine and loftier way!
> Even such this blessèd Pilgrim trod,
> By sorrow lifted towards her God.

Because the suffering of Emily "is permanent . . ./And has the nature of infinity," after her death her beatified spirit survives in the Doe—

> Who, having filled a holy place,
> Partakes, in her degree, Heaven's grace;
> And bears a memory and a mind
> Raised far above the law of kind.

The Doe remains the living emblem of that "fortitude of patience" which looks through finite suffering to infinite salvation.

The question may well be asked why Wordsworth did not have Emily return to society, where her faith might be fulfilled by works. One of Wordsworth's basic purposes in writing his poetry, as attested by his letter to Lady Beaumont at the very period when he was about to begin *The White Doe,* was to console the afflicted. Emily's victory is obviously directed to this purpose; for, by picturing her as having no outward stimulus or reward, except the unquenchable triumph of her own soul, her victory is most completely demonstrated. As Wordsworth says, "Everything that is attempted by the principal personages in *The White Doe* fails, so far as its object is external and substantial. So far as it is moral and spiritual it succeeds."

Emily's valor is set in sharp contrast to that of her father whose heroism is external. But hers is no less militant: she made "a *conquest* over her own sorrows." Wordsworth similarly triumphed in his battle with despair following the death of his brother John. When he came to write *The White Doe,* he dared address himself calmly "to scale the dizzy cliffs of anguish where mortal senses reel" because his own feelings about his brother's death gave him guidance in his ascent. In that soul-searching Wordsworth found the ministry of nature by itself insufficent; hence, he sought support and guidance in religious faith. Having won his own struggle with despondency, Wordsworth, unlike the heroine of Rylstone, directed his hope and ministry to the outer world. But in the years following *The White Doe,* he did so with the increasing help of the teachings of orthodox Christianity.

The Later Poetry

After *The Excursion,* though there appeared not much more that was great and distinctive in his poetry, Wordsworth was always ready to employ new approaches to make his offerings attractive. He sought fresh materials for his poems not only from "natural objects" but from the literature and history of classical times. He also adopted a new metaphorical practice by using his subjects more directly as symbols. At the time he was helping his son John prepared for college, his interest in Greek and Roman mythology revived. The immediate result of this renewed interest was the composition of "Laodamia" and "Dion."

"Laodamia," founded on the description of the underworld in Virgil's *Aeneid,* book 6, was composed while *The Excursion* was being prepared for the press and was first published in *Poems* (1815). This poem, Wordsworth said, "cost me more trouble than almost anything of equal length I have ever written." It tells how Laodamia is allowed by the gods, in answer to her fervent prayer, to converse for a brief space with her husband Protesilaus, the first warrior to die at Troy. When Laodamia sees her husband, she passionately longs to embrace him and revive "the joys of sense." But she is sternly told by Protesilaus to control her rebellious passion: "for the Gods approve/ The depth, and not the tumult, of the soul;/A fervent, not an ungovernable, love." He adjures her to "mourn meekly" and await with patience "Our blest reunion in the shades below."

But Laodamia's passion is too strong. When the wraith is summoned away, in a transport of grief she falls dead on the floor of the palace. Wordsworth, who was deeply moved by the human implications of this tragedy, had great difficulty in settling on a satisfactory ending. In the first printed version he deviated from the myth in letting the overpassionate Laodamia go altogether free from punishment. In 1827, however, he was persuaded to change her doom, in agreement with Virgil, to one more severe: she must wander for eternity "in a grosser clime" in Hades "apart from happy Ghosts." Five years later, Wordsworth relented his severity toward Laodamia and at the last doomed her only "to wear out her appointed time." Thus, he finally settled, much to his credit, for a compromise between myth and his own heart. Like "Laodamia," the story of "Dion" is based on the classics (the source is Plutarch) and, also like it, has an exalted moral strain. When Dion is tempted unjustly to shed human blood, though ostensibly for the public good, the judgment upon him is absolute: "Him, only him, the shield of Jove defends,/Whose means are fair and spotless as his ends."

In 1818, long after Wordsworth had taken his conscious farewell of the "visionary gleam," a radiant sunset seen from the mound in front of his home at Rydal revived in him a momentary glimpse of glory. He tells with an intermingling of joy and pain of the sudden illumination from another world in the well-known lines "Composed upon an Evening of Extraordinary Splendour and Beauty." The experience has close associations with the Immortality Ode. The splendor of the sunset recalls

> the light
> Full early lost, and fruitlessly deplored,
> Which, at this moment, on my waking sight
> Appears to shine, by miracle restored.

However, the "visionary gleam" has an ephemeral luster that quickly fades, and the poem resulting from it really has little of the old magic. Wordsworth first included it with *Poems of Imagination,* but he later transferred it to the group of *Evening Voluntaries.*

By 1819, nature came to provide delightful interludes for the poet rather than to transform experience. A composite of such interludes resulted in a sonnet series describing the Duddon River. The poet had from his youth onward "many affecting remembrances" associated with the stream, and these he weaves together in an imaginary day's ramble from its rise at the top of Wrynose Pass as it ripples, winds, and widens on its way to the sea. In the sonnets recording this ramble Wordsworth is much less concerned with giving pleasure through pictorial images (though these are not lacking) than with providing stirring thoughts to elevate the mind. He intertwines his own private affections, memories, and hopes with the ever-changing landscape; and he joins to them the legendary and historical associations of this lovely stream.

When published in 1820, *The River Duddon* was "more warmly received" than any other of Wordsworth's writings. Most readers found the symbolism easy to understand, and they could enjoy the pleasant human links skillfully made by the poet with the onflowing stream and the pastoral and mountain landscape. Actually, there is nothing especially noteworthy about the thirty-three miscellaneous sonnets marking the river's course to the sea. However, in "After-Thought," in which the poet sums up the symbolic meaning of the poetical journey from mountain to ocean, he has written one of the greatest of all his sonnets. Here time and space are transcended. The river that flows out and loses itself in the sea is the eternal life-force of man's spirit as it emerges from the unknown, runs its earthly course, and merges again with the eternal. It represents the spiritual oneness of man and nature deeply interfused, "what was, and is, and will abide."

Wordsworth was able over the years intuitively to reconcile his visionary views with the doctrine of the Anglican Church without any compromise to either. In 1822 he published *Ecclesiastical Sketches* in which he traces the history of the English church from its beginnings. At no time in this series does he exploit or defend religion; of open didacticism there is hardly a trace. As the poetical chronicle unfolds, Wordsworth stands as "spectator ab extra" watching over the new forces and ways of the Church developing through the centuries. Throughout the sequence, the theme is handled with tolerance and wisdom. In occasional detached or isolated moments there is an inrush of magnificent poetry, like that in which the poet in "King's College Chapel" opens the way to infinity, or in "Mutability" finds that "Truth fails not" but the forms that enshrine her gradually melt "like frosty rime."

During his middle and later years, Wordsworth's love of traveling did not abate; and he often used the objects and experiences of his tours as the subjects for new poems. During the summer of 1814, the poet made a second visit to Scotland with Mary and Sara Hutchinson. In the company of James Hogg he visited Yarrow River and wrote the central piece "Yarrow Visited" in a trilogy that began with "Yarrow Unvisited" in 1803 and ended with "Yarrow Revisited" in 1831.[8] When he first visited the stream, he realized that what he saw in the light of day rivaled the delicate creation of "fond imagination." And, as the sunshine played upon its surface, he was led to anticipate a future joy in the recollection of "Thy genuine image, Yarrow!" The beauty of nature never lost its power to delight the poet in moments recollected in tranquillity. Even after seventeen years had passed and Wordsworth had again beheld the "unaltered face" of the river in the company of Walter Scott and contrasted the change the years had brought to himself and the "Great Minstrel of the Border," he concluded by observing that Yarrow's image was "dearer still to memory's shadowy moonshine."

But "Yarrow Revisited," Wordsworth himself said, was too heavily laden with the pressure of fact for the verses to harmonize satisfactorily with the two preceding poems. Scott was about to set out for Italy in a vain search for health and came back only to die. When the group returned from Yarrow and forded the Tweed to Abbotsford, the sun cast upon the Eildon Hills "a rich but sad light." Wordsworth sensed that it was the last time Scott would cross that beloved river. A few days later he composed a farewell sonnet to Scott, "A trouble, not of clouds, or weeping rain." An equally noble tribute to his friend written at that time also vibrates in the splendid Trossachs sonnet. In 1835, when Wordsworth received news of the death of Hogg, he vividly recalled his visits to Yarrow with the Ettrick Shepherd and Scott, and he composed on the spot a magnificent personal elegy to their memory. Also included in this "Extempore Effusion" were Coleridge, Lamb, Crabbe, and Felicia Hemans, who within the short span of three years, had joined them in "the sunless land."

Wordsworth's fame grew slowly over the years, but in the last decade it almost overwhelmed him. When in 1839 Oxford honored him with a doctorate degree, the ovation that greeted him was one of the most tremendous the university had ever witnessed. On Southey's death in 1843, Wordsworth was made poet laureate. At last he came to realize that the prophetic words he had written long years before in simple confidence to comfort Lady Beaumont were being fulfilled. In that earlier time when his poems were scorned, he bade her to trust that their destiny would be "to console the afflicted; to add sunshine to daylight, by making the happy happier; to teach the young and the gracious of every age to see, to think, and feel, and therefore, to become more actively and securely virtuous." As he hoped, the poems have faithfully performed that service.

In April 1850, full of years and honors, William Wordsworth, one of England's greatest poets, died. He lies buried in the churchyard of Grasmere beneath the shade of yew trees planted by his own hand and in the sound of the incessant murmuring of the mountain stream. So the "ceaseless music" of running water, which at the beginning of life, as he tells the reader, quickened his gift of poetry, accompanies his spirit still. And the music he made flows without ceasing to all who have ears to hear it.

Conclusion

William Wordsworth was the most truly original genius of his age and exerted a power over the poetic destinies of his century unequaled by any of his contemporaries. Wordsworth's originality was recognized early by Coleridge, who, during his last year of residence at Cambridge, became acquainted with *Descriptive Sketches*. "Seldom, if ever," wrote Coleridge in *Biographia Literaria* in remembrance of that occasion, "was the emergence of an original poetic genius above the literary horizon more evidently announced." With the publication of *Lyrical Ballads,* the challenge of the new kind of poetry was quickly acknowledged and accepted by the public at large.

But, if Wordsworth provided an expanded view of what was possible in poetry, he also called forth ridicule and opposition. Francis Jeffrey, who thought that the poet was "too ambitious of originality," held that what he was attempting was wrong-headed. Wordsworth himself foresaw that there would be resistance, but he did not foresee the extent of it, and cautioned readers that they would "perhaps frequently have to struggle with feelings of strangeness and awkwardness." For two decades Jeffrey did not relent in his attack on Wordsworth, but the poet remained to the end unshaken in the rightness of his poetic innovations.

In his considered statement on the subject of the poet's creative freedom ("Essay Supplementary to the Preface," 1815), Wordsworth observes in a passage often quoted, that, insofar as a poet is great and "at the same time original," he has the task of creating the taste by which he will be enjoyed; the great poet will, therefore, "clear and often shape his own road." Francis Jeffrey succeeded in slowing down public acceptance of Wordsworth; but, by the early 1820s, by virtue of his own great strength the poet had gained such headway with the public that his genius won recognition despite adverse criticism. Thereafter the opposition among critics and readers alike quickly faded, and Wordsworth's fame steadily rose until it reached a high point in the 1830s. In his declining years Wordsworth was acknowledged as the preeminent living British poet, and when he died he was honored and revered by a wide public. Shortly after his death, his popularity receded somewhat and reached an ebb around 1865.

In the late 1870s a highly significant essay by Leslie Stephen provoked a famous reply by Matthew Arnold, which stimulated new interest in

Wordsworth among scholars and general readers. Since Arnold's time, critical studies and biographies have multiplied; and readers have grown in numbers with the years. Today, there are few responsible critics who would question Wordsworth's right to a place among the foremost English poets. Wordsworth does not, to be sure, meet with the ready acceptance accorded Chaucer and Shakespeare. There is a certain pedestrian tone in some of the poems, an unfortunate element of prosiness that is easy to laugh at. Often matter-of-fact, even banal, details are inextricably intertwined in his works with the most inspired and sublime passages. Coleridge and others since have complained of the inconstancy and disharmony of Wordsworth's style.

Some readers have also been unhappy about his compulsion to moralize. But Wordsworth wished to be thought of as a teacher or as nothing. In this role he might have found more ready acceptance if he had been mindful of Dryden's golden maxim (a maxim he accepts in theory) that poesy only instructs as it delights. He might have employed more often than he did a light touch of humor, but he generally eschews that saving grace. Some readers have felt that Wordsworth lacked the gift of dramatic imagination and, in some respects, the storyteller's art. But, granting a good deal, even granting that in some of Wordsworth's best work there are occasional flaws that are difficult to excuse, there yet remains a massive body of poetry written at the height of his powers with an immense variety of excellences and a wide and unfading appeal.

The greatness of Wordsworth's best work proceeds from a calm, almost elemental, strength. He possessed a weight of character, an extraordinary emotional force and reach of intellect, and a tremendous imaginative power. The source of his strength lay within his own extraordinary powers of awareness. He saw things that other people do not see, or see but dimly, and he saw them with singular frequency and vividness. His poetic impulse came to him through some perfectly familiar experience, such as beholding the rainbow or hearing the shout of the cuckoo. From an impression simply and purely sensuous, he would establish a mood of mind or feeling in which, as R. D. Havens has written, "the object contemplated was suddenly released from the tie of custom and became a source of mysterious exaltation." In such brief, intensely charged moments Wordsworth experienced a feeling of release; sensation blanked out, consciousness was almost completely lost, and he became a "living soul." Through frequent repetitions of these periods of vision, Wordsworth became overpoweringly aware of the reality and importance of the spiritual world. This spiritual world, however, is not an isolated state but the sensible world more fully apprehended. Everything is apocalyptic, but everything, too, is natural. An auxiliary light from the mind bestowed new splendor on the forms and colors of earth. In the view of a Victorian critic, a "wonderful interchange" went on between the poet and everything about him, "they flowing into him, he going out to them. His soul attracted them to itself, as a mountaintop draws the clouds, and at their touch woke up to feel its kinship with the mysterious life that is in all nature and in each separate object of nature."[1]

Wordsworth is the poet of many things besides, but it is in his relation to nature that his poetic inspiration originates. It was among the "grand and permanent forms" of nature that he most unmistakably *felt* the wisdom and spirit of the universe. It was there that his faith in the dignity and independence of man was confirmed. Through both man and nature alike there rolls the divine something "more deeply interfused." The mergence of the human figure with nature gave it that degree of dignity and virtue that alone would allow it to become, for Wordsworth, a worthy symbol of human life. Wordsworth's typical human figures—the Solitary Reaper, the Wanderer, Lucy, the Old Cumberland Beggar—are those who are most intimately "engaged" with their natural surroundings. His most authentic voice sounds in those passages where man and nature are bound together in natural piety.

The mind of man "wedded to this goodly universe/In love and holy passion" is the haunt, and the main region, of Wordsworth's song. He probes the deepest secrets of the human mind and heart, whether in rapturous communion or in heroic conflict. In his most significant work he is a psychologist who deals with "the primary laws of our nature" and the fundamental passions. But he is psychological, not pathological. When he treats of sex, it is in a normal and healthful fashion. His lines to Annette, for example, are elemental and moving:

> The house she dwelt in was a sainted shrine
> Her chamber-window did surpass in glory
> The portals of the East, all paradise
> Could by the simple opening of a door,
> Let itself in upon him.

There is nothing distortingly pathological about these verses. They are primary, nobly plain, wholesomely sincere. As Arnold said, they have the permanence of "what is really life." Wordsworth's preoccupation is with a distinctively human naturalness; a sanity and spiritual health lay at the core of his poetry and lasted a lifetime.

His interest in psychology caused him often to choose peasants, children, defectives, and old people as means of searching the human spirit for those universal laws that govern every man's being. With true sympathy and profound imaginative insight he has reached into the humblest hearts and discovered in the primary affections a true source of joy and strength for living. Out of a boy's random feelings, a mother's sorrow, or a leech-gatherer's talk about his trade he framed his songs, which rise from lowliest origins to the universality and nobility of Greek tragedy. Wordsworth's deepest concern was for the betterment of mankind through a fuller, happier realization of hidden resources within each individual.

Wordsworth is still in the great Renaissance tradition that looked upon the poet as a responsible human spokesman. He was the guardian of the social health. "There is scarcely one of my poems which does not aim to direct attention to some moral sentiment," he writes to Lady Beaumont. He purposes "to console the afflicted . . . to teach the young," to make man "wiser, better, and happier." Doomed, as all men are, "to go in company with Pain, and Fear," he learned to bear the shocks of life with honor and turned grief to account. He felt that poems could alter persons and bring health to society. Where health was departing from society, it was the poet's duty to call society back. Wordsworth's unique experiences, particularly his residence in France during the Revolution, as well as his genius, gave him an unequaled perspective for interpreting the essential thoughts and passions of his age. In the political realm, he was led to hope—not mistakenly, as it proved—that his countrymen might be roused by an appeal to the ideals of freedom to a renewed sense of their strength and their responsibility.

Wordsworth's insight led him to perfect a new kind of poetry which gave a forward impetus to English and American thought and expression that has hardly yet subsided. His diction and style, as Coleridge long ago pointed out, is peculiarly his own and "cannot be imitated, without its being at once recognized as originating in Mr. Wordsworth." At its best, his style is unsurpassed in its naked idiomatic force and its quiet unadorned beauty of word and phrase. It excels in epigrammatic power, dignity, ampleness, poignant intensity, and vigorous masculinity. Wordsworth is not at all a monotonous poet but exhibits a great variety in style, mood, and subject matter. Among the short lyrics alone there is a long roll call of perennial favorites displaying his extraordinary variety in form and range of material. Nor does Wordsworth lack a sense of humor, as it was for a long time fashionable to believe. Much of his humor might be called "a joyous parody of life" and is characteristically droll; much of it "comes from a twisting of simplicity, seeing the humble in a warm or wry light."[2] As for variety and vitality of pure poetic expression, "Where," asks Mr. Herbert Read, "can you match the wealth of Shakespeare except in Wordsworth?"

Wordsworth is preeminent for the truth of his report about nature and he is one of the great poets of the human heart. His poetry has penetrated beyond the show of things to the realm of the universal. As a poet gifted with "the Vision and the Faculty divine," he has seized upon those profound spiritual relationships that exist among man, nature, and the eternal world. Some of the truths advanced by Wordsworth that appeared startlingly new to his generation and were revered by the Victorians may no longer seem pertinent in our secular age. Some portions of his report on nature may need qualifying. But one would not willingly yield the gains he has won for mankind. He has handed on an impressive body of philosophical speculation that stimulates thought and challenges meditation.

Indeed, his observations have a strikingly modern bearing: "For a multitude of causes, unknown to former times, are now acting with a combined force to blunt the discriminating powers of the mind, and, . . . to reduce it to a state of almost savage torpor. The most effective of these causes are the great national events which are daily taking place, and the increasing accumulation of men in cities, where the uniformity of their occupations produces a craving for extraordinary incident, which the rapid communication of intelligence hourly gratifies."[3] For many a sufferer looking up from the dark Satanic mills of the twentieth century, Wordsworth has the "healing power" to fortify the spirit. He endures because of the great power with which he transmits the joy offered in nature, and the joy offered all men and women in the simple affections and duties of their daily lives.

Notes and References

Chapter One

1. Fenwick note, Ernest de Selincourt and Helen Darbishire, eds., *The Poetical Works of William Wordsworth* (Oxford: Clarendon Press, 1940–49), 1:319. All subsequent citations of Wordsworth's poems are from this edition.

2. Z. S. Fink, in *The Early Wordsworthian Milieu* (Oxford: Clarendon Press, 1958), 23–42, has shown how Wordsworth refashioned incidents and images from his personal experience in the Lake Country to the traditional purposes of the topographical poem without ever sacrificing the factual to the picturesque.

3. In the "sunset storm" passage (*Descriptive Sketches,* 332–47), there is an isolated instance in which Wordsworth reaches inner vision—not through a blending of images of sight but through a supercharged excess of them. For a discussion of this passage and the problems relating to Wordsworth's imaginative vision, see G. H. Hartman, "Wordsworth's *Descriptive Sketches* and the Growth of the Poet's Mind," *Publications of the Modern Language Association,* 76 (1961):519–27.

4. There is a good deal of evidence that Wordsworth was an active radical during his time in London. See Nicholas Roe, *Wordsworth and Coleridge: The Radical Years* (Oxford: Oxford University Press, 1988).

5. S. T. Coleridge, *Biographia Literaria,* ed. James Engell and W. Jackson Bate (London: Routledge & Kegan Paul, 1983), chap. 4.

6. Wordsworth's contact with the radical circle of his publisher, Joseph Johnson, would have made him well acquainted with Godwin's writings.

7. *The Prelude* (1805), 10:806–830.

8. *The Early Letters of William and Dorothy Wordsworth,* 2d ed., ed. Ernest de Selincourt (Oxford: Clarendon Press, 1967), 124.

9. Wordsworth and Godwin saw much of each other in 1795 when Godwin was at the height of his fame. The two men met and corresponded with something like regularity until Godwin's death in 1836.

10. See Robert Osborn's comments in *Bicentenary Wordsworth Studies* (Ithaca, N.Y: Cornell University Press, 1970), 399–400; Charles Smith also argues the point in *Studies in Philology* 50 (1953):631–32.

11. The essay and preface can be found in *The Prose Works of William Wordsworth,* ed. W. J. B. Owen and J. W. Smyser (Oxford: Clarendon Press, 1974). The Fenwick note is contained in *Poems* 1:342–43.

12. John F. Danby, *The Simple Wordsworth* (London: Routledge, 1960), 77.

13. "The Ruined Cottage," completed at Racedown in the spring of 1797, was revised and expanded in February 1798 and eventually became the first book of *The Excursion.*

14. G. W. Meyer, *Wordsworth's Formative Years* (Ann Arbor: University of Michigan Press, 1943), 246.

Chapter Two

1. Coleridge to Lady Beaumont, 3 April 1815, *Collected Letters of Samuel Taylor Coleridge,* ed. E. L. Griggs (Oxford: Clarendon Press, 1956–71), 4:564 (hereafter cited as *Collected Letters*).
2. Coleridge to Joseph Cottle, 8 June 1797, *Collected Letters,* 1:325.
3. Christopher Wordsworth, *Memoirs of William Wordsworth* (London: Moxon, 1851), 2:288–89.
4. William Wordsworth to Francis Wrangham, 5 June 1808, *The Letters of William and Dorothy Wordsworth: The Middle Years,* vol. 1, ed. Ernest de Selincourt (Oxford: Clarendon Press, 1937), 248.
5. John Jordan identifies eleven poems as experimental in *Why the Lyrical Ballads?* (Berkeley: University of California Press, 1976), 35.
6. Robert Mayo, "The Contemporaneity of the *Lyrical Ballads,*" *Publications of the Modern Language Association* 69 (1954):495.
7. Helen Darbishire, *The Poet Wordsworth* (Oxford: Clarendon Press, 1950), 61.
8. S. M. Parrish, "Dramatic Technique in the *Lyrical Ballads,*" *Publications of the Modern Language Association* 74 (1959):85–97.
9. John F. Danby, *The Simple Wordsworth* (London: Routledge, 1960), 50.
10. Coleridge, *Biographia Literaria,* ed. Shawcross, vol. 2, p. 35.
11. "My First Acquaintance with Poets," 1823, in *The Complete Works of William Hazlitt,* ed. P. P. Howe (London: J. M. Dent, 1930–34), 17:118.
12. The following passage in Gilpin should be compared with "Tintern Abbey": "Many of the furnaces, on the banks of the river, consume charcoal, which is manufactured on the spot; and the smoke, which is frequently seen issuing from the sides of the hills; and spreading its thin veil over a part of them, beautifully breaks their lines, and unites them with the sky." For the other echoes in the poem, see John O. Hayden, "The Road to Tintern Abbey," *The Wordsworth Circle* 12 (1981):211–16.

Chapter Three

1. "I Travelled among Unknown Men" was composed in April 1801 after Wordsworth's return to England, but it recreates perfectly the nostalgic love of his own country felt during the winter at Goslar.
2. Cf. the lines from "Tintern Abbey": "that serene and blessed mood/In which . . . we are laid asleep in body, and become a living soul . . . [and] see into the life of things."
3. *The Ruined Cottage and The Pedlar,* ed. James Butler (Ithaca, N.Y.: Cornell University Press, 1979), 382–414.

4. Wordsworth to Thomas Poole, 9 April 1801, *Early Letters,* 322.

5. Mary Moorman, *William Wordsworth: The Early Years* (Oxford: Clarendon Press, 1957), 500.

6. Samuel Taylor Coleridge to William Sotheby, *Collected Letters,* 2:444.

7. See John O. Hayden, "Wordsworth and Coleridge: Shattered Mirrors, Shining Lamps?" *Wordsworth Circle* 12 (1981):71–81.

8. M. H. Abrams, *The Mirror and the Lamp* (New York: Oxford University Press, 1953), chap. 1.

9. *Early Letters* (7 June 1802), 355–58, and (14 January 1801), 315; *Complete Prose Works of Matthew Arnold,* ed. R. S. Super (Ann Arbor: University of Michigan Press, 1973), 9:44–45.

Chapter Four

1. David Ellis argues, on the contrary, that Wordsworth was striving for autobiographical precision. See his *Wordsworth, Freud, and the Spots of Time* (Cambridge: Cambridge University Press, 1985), 10–11.

2. All references to *The Prelude* are to the Norton Edition, ed. Jonathan Wordsworth et al. (New York: W. W. Norton, 1979), and the references are to the 1805 text unless otherwise stated.

3. See, for example, book 1:490–94:

> Ye Presences of Nature, in the sky
> And on the earth! Ye visions of the hills!
> And Souls of lonely places! can I think
> A vulgar hope was yours when Ye employ'd
> Such ministry.

4. See, for example, book 1:614–40.

5. Cf. "Tintern Abbey," 45–49:

> . . . we are laid asleep
> In body, and become a living soul:
> While with an eye made quiet by the power
> Of harmony, and the deep power of joy,
> We see into the life of things.

6. See Wordsworth's elaboration of the point to De Quincey in Thomas De Quincey, *Literary Reminiscences* (Boston: Ticknor, Reed, and Fields, 1851–60), 1:308–309.

7. Herbert Lindenberger, *On Wordsworth's "Prelude,"* (Princeton, N.J.: Princeton University Press, 1963), 28–38.

8. See Francis Christensen, "Intellectual Love: The Second Theme of *The Prelude*," *Publications of the Modern Language Association* 80 (1965): 69–75.

9. Cf. Lindenberger, 209–219.

10. Wordsworth to Sir George Beaumont, 1 May 1805. *Early Letters*, 586.

11. Introduction to the first edition of *The Prelude*, ed. de Selincourt, 1926, xxvii.

12. See book 8:594–605.

13. See Davie's chapter on the syntax of Wordsworth's *Prelude* in his *Articulate Energy* (New York: Harcourt, Brace & Co., 1955), 106–116.

14. See, for example, book 8: 119–45, which is strongly reminiscent in style, construction, and phrasing of *Paradise Lost*, 4:208–247. For additional illustrations of Milton's influence, consult R. D. Havens, *The Mind of a Poet* (Baltimore: Johns Hopkins University Press, 1941), Index "Milton," 652.

Chapter Five

1. The poem can be found in William Wordsworth: The Poems, ed. John O. Hayden (Penguin, 1977). On the matter of authenticity, see Jonathan Wordsworth, *College English* 27 (1966): 455–65, and John Beer et al., *Review of English Studies* 37 (1986): 348–83.

2. *Early Letters*, 366.

3. In a letter to Anne Taylor, he said he intended, "If my health will permit me, to devote my life to literature." See *Early Letters*, 327. Wordsworth aged early; his spirit and energy perhaps burned him out. He seems to be anticipating the loss of his powers in strophe 7.

4. Ernest de Selincourt, ed., *Journals of Dorothy Wordsworth* (London: Macmillan, 1941), 1:286.

5. Some of the lines addressed to the Highland girl overflowed and became the germ of "She was a Phantom of delight," the poet's lovely tribute to his wife.

6. T. M. Raysor "The Themes of Immortality and Natural Piety in Wordsworth's Immortality Ode," *Publications of the Modern Language Association* 69 (1954):861–75.

7. Alan Grob, "Wordsworth's Immortality Ode and the Search for Identity," *Journal of English Literary History* 32 (1965): 32–61.

8. Cf., for example, A. C. Bradley, *Oxford Lectures on Poetry* (London: Macmillan, 1909), 129–41; Arthur Beatty, *William Wordsworth* (Madison: University of Wisconsin Press, 1922), 84–86; and Lionel Trilling, *The Liberal Imagination* (New York: Viking, 1950), 129–53.

9. See Mary Moorman, *William Wordsworth: The Early Years* (Oxford: Clarendon Press, 1957) 526.

10. Coleridge was early attracted to Neoplatonic speculations on preexistence and degraded intelligences and had written a sonnet on the birth of his son Hartley expressing a feeling, which he often had, that "the present has appeared like a vivid

dream or exact similitude of some *past* circumstance" (letter to Thomas Poole, 1 November 1796).

11. Wordsworth says that "two years at least passed between the writing of the four first stanzas and the remaining parts." But he was often mistaken about the dating of his poems. An impressive body of evidence has been brought together showing that Wordsworth composed most, if not all, of the stanzas on preexistence in the early summer of 1802. For a full reporting of the evidence, see John D. Rea, "Coleridge's Intimations of Immortality from Proclus," *Modern Philology* 26 (1928): 201–213, and Herbert Hartman, "The 'Intimations' in Wordsworth's 'Ode,' " *Review of English Studies* 6 (1930): 129–48.

12. See D. A. Stauffer, "Cooperative Criticism," *Kenyon Review* 4 (1942): 133–44.

13. See Mary Moorman, *William Wordsworth: The Later Years* (Oxford: Clarendon Press, 1965), 1–7.

14. The poet has in mind Mary Hutchinson as he described her in *The Prelude* (1850), 12:155–58.

Chapter Six

1. See chapter 4 for an account of these revisions.

2. Coleridge wished his friend to address a poem "to those, who, in consequence of the complete failure of the French Revolution have thrown up all hopes of the amelioration of mankind, and are sinking into an almost epicurean selfishness, disguising the same under the soft titles of domestic attachment and contempt for visionary *philosophes.*" See Christopher Wordsworth, *Memoirs of William Wordsworth*, 1:159.

3. For a full account and appraisal of the story of Margaret, see chapter 1.

4. J. S. Lyon, *The Excursion: A Study* (New Haven: Yale University Press, 1950), 140 (and for a detailed analysis of this poem's structure and style, pp. 122–38).

5. *Memoirs,* 2:311.

6. See James A. W. Heffernan, "Wordsworth on Imagination: The Emblemizing Power," *Publications of the Modern Language Association* 81 (1966):394. Heffernan offers an excellent interpretation of *The White Doe.*

7. *Letters: The Middle Years,* 1:222.

8. See chapter 5 for a discussion of "Yarrow Unvisited."

Conclusion

1. J. C. Shairp, *Studies in Poetry and Philosophy* (Edinburgh: D. Douglas, 1868).

2. See. J. E. Jordan's "Wordsworth's Humor," *Publications of the Modern Language Association* 63 (1958): 81–93.

3. Preface to *Lyrical Ballads,* 1800.

Selected Bibliography

PRIMARY WORKS

Collections of Poems

The Poetical Works of William Wordsworth. Edited by Ernest de Selincourt and Helen Darbishire. 5 vols. Oxford: Clarendon Press, 1940–49. A second edition of volumes 1–3 was issued by Darbishire, 1952–54.

The Poetical Works of William Wordsworth. Edited by Thomas Hutchinson. New York: Oxford University Press, 1911. Revised by Ernest de Selincourt, 1950. The standard, one-volume edition with Wordsworth's arrangement of the poems.

William Wordsworth. Edited by Stephen Gill. Oxford: Oxford University Press, 1984. Selected poems in their earliest completed state.

William Wordsworth: The Poems. Edited by John O. Hayden. 2 vols. Harmondsworth: Penguin, 1977. Contains all poems, except *The Prelude,* and includes several previously unpublished. Poems are given with annotations, in chronological order by date of composition.

Lyrical Ballads. Edited by R. L. Brett and A. R. Jones. London: Methuen, 1963. The text of the 1798 edition with the additional 1800 poems and preface. With an introduction and notes.

The Prelude, or Growth of a Poet's Mind. Edited by Ernest de Selincourt. Oxford: Clarendon, 1926. 2d edition, revised by Helen Darbishire, 1959. The text of 1805 is printed opposite the text of 1850, with variant readings, notes, and commentary. Text superseded by the edition of Jonathan Wordsworth et al.

William Wordsworth: "The Prelude," A Parallel Text. Edited by J. C. Maxwell. Harmondsworth: Penguin, 1971.

The Prelude: 1799, 1805, 1850. Edited by Jonathan Wordsworth, M. H. Abrams, and Stephen Gill. New York: W. W. Norton, 1979. A Norton Critical edition giving authoritative texts of the three versions of the poem, context and reception, and recent critical essays.

The Cornell Wordsworth. General Editors, Stephen Parrish, Mark L. Reed, and James A. Butler. Ithaca, N.Y.: Cornell University Press, in progress:

> *The Salisbury Plain Poems.* Edited by Stephen Gill, 1975.
> *The Prelude, 1798–1799.* Edited by Stephen Parrish, 1977.
> *Home at Grasmere.* Edited by Beth Darlington, 1977.
> *The Ruined Cottage and The Pedlar.* Edited by James Butler, 1979.
> *Benjamin the Waggoner.* Edited by Paul F. Betz, 1981.

The Borderers. Edited by Robert Osborn, 1982.

Poems in Two Volumes, and Other Poems, 1800–1807. Edited by Jared
   Curtis, 1983.

An Evening Walk. Edited by James Averill, 1984.

Descriptive Sketches. Edited by Eric Birdsall, with the assistance of Paul
   M. Zall, 1984.

Peter Bell. Edited by John E. Jordan, 1985.

The Fourteen-Book "Prelude." Edited by W. J. B. Owen, 1985.

"The Tuft of Primroses" with Other Late Poems for "The Recluse." Edited
   by Joseph F. Kishel, 1986.

The White Doe of Rylstone. Edited by Kristine Dugas, 1988.

The Ecclesiastical Sonnets of William Wordsworth. Edited by Abbie Findlay Potts.
   New Haven: Yale University Press, 1922. Discusses manuscripts, composition, and structure of the series. Copious notes.

Prose and Letters

The Prose Works of William Wordsworth. Edited by W. J. B. Owen and Jane
   Worthington Smyser. 3 Vols. Oxford: Clarendon Press, 1974. Each prose
   work is provided with introduction and commentary. Vol. 3 has an index.
   Supersedes Grosart's incomplete and inaccurate edition (1896), which does,
   however, include a section of reported conversations.

William Wordsworth: Selected Prose. Edited by John O. Hayden. Harmondsworth:
   Penguin, 1988. Contains most of Wordsworth's prose pieces, with introduc-
   tions and notes.

Wordsworth's Preface to Lyrical Ballads. Edited by W. J. B. Owen, with an introduction and commentary. Copenhagen: Rosenkilde and Bagger, 1957.

Journals of Dorothy Wordsworth. Edited by Ernest de Selincourt. 2 vols. London:
   Macmillan, 1952. A new edition of two early journals, edited by Mary
   Moorman, was published by Oxford University Press (Oxford, 1971).

The Early Letters of William and Dorothy Wordsworth: (1787–1805). Edited by
   Ernest de Selincourt. Oxford: Clarendon, 1935. 2d ed., revised by Chester L.
   Shaver, 1967.

The Letters of William and Dorothy Wordsworth: The Middle Years. Arranged and
   edited by E. de Selincourt. 2 vols. Oxford: Clarendon, 1937. Second edition,
   part 1, 1806–11, revised by Mary Moorman, 1969; part 2, 1812–20, revised by Mary Moorman and Alan G. Hill, 1970.

The Letters of William and Dorothy Wordsworth: The Later Years. Edited by Ernest
   de Selincourt. 3 vols. Oxford: Clarendon, 1939. Part 1, 2d ed., 1821–28,
   part 2, 1829–34, part 3, 1835–39, revised by Alan G. Hill, 1978, 1979,
   1982.

The Love Letters of William and Mary Wordsworth. Edited by Beth Darlington.
   Ithaca, N.Y.: Cornell University Press, 1981.

SECONDARY WORKS

Bibliographies

Bauer, N. S. *William Wordsworth: A Reference Guide to British Criticism, 1793–1899.* Boston: G. K. Hall, 1978. Annotated bibliography with index.

Fogle, Richard Harter. *Romantic Poets and Prose Writers.* New York: Appleton-Century-Crofts, 1967. In the Goldentree Bibliography series: contains useful short bibliography of Wordsworth.

Healey, George H. *The Cornell Wordsworth Collection: A Catalogue.* Ithaca, N.Y.: Cornell University Press, 1957. Useful for information about early editions and primary documents.

Henley, Elton F., and **David H. Stam.** *Wordsworthian Criticism, 1945–1964: An Annotated Bibliography.* New York: New York Public Library, 1965. Continues the work begun by Logan.

Jones, Mark, and **Karl Kroeber.** *Wordsworth Scholarship and Criticism, 1973–1984: An Annotated Bibliography with Selected Criticism, 1809–1972.* New York: Garland, 1985. Continues where Stam left off.

Logan, James V. *Wordsworthian Criticism: A Guide and Bibliography.* Columbus: Ohio State University Press, 1947. Reprinted 1961. Annotated bibliography with an introductory chapter on Wordsworth's critical reputation.

Raysor, Thomas M. Editor. *The English Romantic Poets: A Review of Research.* New York: Modern Language Association. Fourth edition revised by Frank Jordan, 1985.

Stam, David H. *Wordsworthian Criticism, 1964–1973: An Annotated Bibliography.* New York: New York Public Library, 1974.

The student should also consult: (1) *The Romantic Movement: A Selective and Critical Bibliography,* ed. D. V. Erdman et al. New York: Garland (1980–), published annually; (2) the annual bibliography of the Romantic movement in *English Language Notes* (1966–79), formerly in *Philological Quarterly* (1950–65) and before that in *English Literary History* (1937–49) [collected in *The Romantic Movement Bibliography, 1936–1970,* ed. A. C. Elkins et al., 7 vols., Ann Arbor: Pieran Press, 1973]; (3) the annual bibliographies in *Publications of the Modern Language Association* and in the Modern Humanities Research Association's *Annual Bibliography of English Language and Literature;* (4) volume 3 of *The New Cambridge Bibliography of English Literature,* 1969.

Biography

Batho, Edith C. *The Later Wordsworth.* Cambridge: Cambridge University Press, 1933. Reprinted, New York: Russell and Russell, 1963. A detailed study of Wordsworth after 1805.

De Selincourt, Ernest. *Dorothy Wordsworth: A Biography.* Oxford: Clarendon Press, 1933.

Gill, Stephen. *William Wordsworth: A Life.* Oxford: Clarendon Press, 1989. The new standard biography.

Gittings, Robert, and **Jo Manton.** *Dorothy Wordsworth.* Oxford: Clarendon, 1985. The standard biography.

Halliday, F. E. *Wordsworth and His World.* London: Thames & Hudson, 1970. Useful short illustrated life.

Harper, George M. *William Wordsworth: His Life, Works, and Influence.* 2 vols. New York: Scribner's, 1916. A revised, abridged edition appeared in 1929. Once the standard biography.

Margoliouth, H. M. *Wordsworth and Coleridge, 1795–1834.* London: Oxford University Press, 1953. Compact, well-balanced account of the celebrated friendship between the two poets.

Moorman, Mary. *William Wordsworth: A Biography.* Vol. 1, *The Early Years, 1770–1803.* Oxford: Clarendon, 1957. A second volume entitled *The Later Years, 1803–1850,* was published in 1965. Once the standard biography, it is now superseded by Stephen Gill's.

Reed, Mark L. *Wordsworth: The Chronology of the Early Years, 1770–1799.* Cambridge, Mass.: Harvard University Press, 1966. A second volume covering the chronology of the middle years, 1800–15, was published in 1975. For the later years, see F. B. Pinion, *A Wordsworth Chronology.* London: Macmillan, 1988.

Roe, Nicholas. *Wordsworth and Coleridge: The Radical Years.* Oxford: Clarendon Press, 1988. Attempts to place Wordsworth's early radical political views in historical context but tends to overemphasize their influence later.

Shaver, Chester L., and **Alice C. Shaver.** *Wordsworth's Library: A Catalogue.* New York: Garland, 1979. A valuable aid in identifying Wordsworth's reading.

Thompson, T. W. *Wordsworth's Hawkshead.* London: Oxford University Press, 1970. A valuable tool for understanding Wordsworth's early life.

Criticism: General

Abrams, M. H. Editor. *Wordsworth: A Collection of Critical Essays.* Englewood Cliffs, N.J.: Prentice-Hall, 1972. Sixteen reprinted essays, ranging from Whitehead and Trilling to Danby and Hartman.

Arnold, Matthew. "Wordsworth." In *The Complete Prose Works of Matthew Arnold,* edited by R. H. Super, 4:36–55. Ann Arbor: University of Michigan Press, 1973. Influential short study of Wordsworth originally published in 1879.

Averill, James H. *Wordsworth and the Poetry of Human Suffering.* Ithaca, N.Y.: Cornell University Press, 1980. Illuminates the influence of the eighteenth-century sentimental movement on Wordsworth, but tends to exaggerate the role of suffering in the poetry after 1797.

Baker, Jeffrey. *Time and Mind in Wordsworth's Poetry.* Detroit: Wayne State University Press, 1980. Discusses Wordsworth's use of four levels of time.

Bateson, F. W. *Wordsworth: A Re-Interpretation.* London: Longmans, 1954; 2d ed., 1956. Stimulating criticism, but marred by unconvincing theorizing of an "incestuous" relationship between the poet and his sister.

Beatty, Arthur. *William Wordsworth: His Doctrine and Art in Their Historical Relations.* Madison: University of Wisconsin Press, 1927. Emphasizes Wordsworth's indebtedness to eighteenth-century thought but is mistaken about the influence of David Hartley. See *Studies in Philology* 81 (1984): 94–118.

Chandler, James K. *Wordsworth's Second Nature: A Study of the Poetry and Politics.* Chicago: University of Chicago Press, 1984. Emphasizes the influence of Edmund Burke.

Clarke, Colin C. *Romantic Paradox: An Essay on the Poetry of Wordsworth.* New York: Barnes & Noble, 1963. Wordsworth's poetry has a far richer texture and is more loaded with ambivalent meanings than has hitherto been recognized.

Coleridge, Samuel T. *Biographia Literaria,* edited by James Engell and W. Jackson Bate. London: Routledge & Kegan Paul, 1983. Chapters 4, 14, and 17–20 are important sources for Wordsworth's poetical theory and practice.

Cowell, Raymond. Editor. *Critics on Wordsworth.* London: George Allen & Unwin, 1973. Collects early and modern criticisms.

Curtis, Jared R. *Wordsworth's Experiments with Tradition: The Lyric Poems of 1802.* Ithaca: Cornell University Press, 1971. Describes the composition of thirty-odd lyric poems and provides the earliest manuscript texts.

Danby, John F. *The Simple Wordsworth: Studies in the Poems, 1797–1807.* London: Routledge, 1960; New York: Barnes & Noble, 1961. Useful for the sensitive reading of some of the "simple" poems: "The Fountain," "The Solitary Reaper," and "The White Doe."

Davies, Hugh Sykes. *Wordsworth and the Worth of Words.* Cambridge: Cambridge University Press, 1986. Analyzes the strategy and uses of Wordsworth's special vocabulary.

Davis, Jack, ed. *Discussions of William Wordsworth.* Boston: D. C. Heath, 1963. Representative selection of the best criticism of Wordsworth by Coleridge, Arnold, Bradley, Willey, Abrams, Leavis, and others.

Dunklin, Gilbert T., ed. *Wordsworth: Centenary Studies Presented at Cornell and Princeton Universities.* Princeton, N.J.: Princeton University Press, 1951. The poet reappraised in studies by Douglas Bush, Frederick A. Pottle, Earl Leslie Griggs, John Crowe Ransom, B. Ifor Evans, Lionel Trilling, and Willard L. Sperry.

Durrant, Geoffrey. *Wordsworth and the Great System: A Study of Wordsworth's Poetic Universe.* Cambridge: Cambridge University Press, 1970. Wordsworth's Newtonian worldview.

Ferry, David. *The Limits of Mortality: An Essay on Wordsworth's Major Poems.*
Middletown Conn.: Wesleyan University Press, 1959. Challenging study;
will doubtless provoke disagreement at times. See, as a corrective, Alan Grob,
"Wordsworth's *Nutting,*" *Journal of English and Germanic Philology* 61
(1962): 826–32.

Grob, Alan. *The Philosophic Mind: A Study of Wordsworth's Poetry and Thought,
1797–1805.* Columbus: Ohio State University Press, 1973. Traces
Wordsworth's philosophical development during the great decade.

Hartman, Geoffrey H. *Wordsworth's Poetry, 1787–1814.* New Haven and London: Yale University Press, 1964. Contains useful bibliographies of criticism.

Hayden, John O. *Polestar of the Ancients: The Aristotelian Tradition in Classical
and English Literary Criticism.* Newark: University of Delaware Press, 1979.
Contains a chapter on the literary theory of Wordsworth and Coleridge.

_____.*The Romantic Reviewers, 1802–1824.* Chicago: University of Chicago
Press, 1969. Contains a chapter on the contemporary reception of
Wordsworth, Coleridge, and Southey.

Heath, William. *Wordsworth and Coleridge: A Study of Their Literary Relations
in 1801–1802.* Oxford: Clarendon, 1970.

Heffernan, James A. W. *Wordsworth's Theory of Poetry.* Ithaca N.Y.: Cornell
University Press, 1969. Analyzes Wordsworth's poetic theory and elucidates
his concept of imagination.

Hodgson, John A. *Wordsworth's Philosophical Poetry, 1797–1814.* Lincoln: University of Nebraska Press, 1980. Deals with five philosophical "stages" from
The Borderers to *The Excursion.*

Johnson, Lee M. *Wordsworth and the Sonnet.* Copenhagen: Rosenkilde & Bagger,
1973. Wordsworth as an important practitioner of the sonnet.

Johnston, Kenneth R., and **Gene W. Ruoff.** Editors. *The Age of William
Wordsworth: Critical Essays on the Romantic Tradition.* New Brunswick:
Rutgers University Press, 1987. Collection of very recent essays centering on
Wordsworth, by a variety of scholars.

Jones, [Henry] John. *The Egotistical Sublime: A History of Wordsworth's Imagination.* London: Chatto & Windus, 1954. Examines the development of
Wordsworth's creative mind.

Marsh, Florence. *Wordsworth's Imagery: A Study in Poetic Vision.* New Haven: Yale
University Press, 1952. An examination of Wordsworth's imagery and style.

Noyes, Russell. *Wordsworth and Jeffrey in Controversy.* Bloomington: Indiana
University Press, 1941. Historical account of the *Edinburgh Review* editor's
attack on the poet and its consequences.

_____. *Wordsworth and the Art of Landscape.* Bloomington: Indiana University
Press, 1968.

Owen, W. J. B. *Wordsworth as Critic.* Toronto: University of Toronto Press, 1969.

Perkins, David. *Wordsworth and the Poetry of Sincerity.* Cambridge, Mass.:
Harvard University Press, 1964. Criticism of a considerable body of Words-

worth's poetry. See also this author's chapter on Wordsworth in *The Quest for Permanence*. Cambridge, Mass.: Harvard University Press, 1959.

Rader, Melvin. *Presiding Ideas of Wordsworth's Poetry. University of Washington Publications in Language and Literature,* 1931. Vol. 8 no. 2. One of the most valuable studies of Wordsworth's Idealism. Revised and enlarged as *Wordsworth: A Philosophical Approach.* Oxford: Clarendon Press, 1967.

Reiman, Donald H., ed. *The Romantics Reviewed: Contemporary Reviews of British Romantic Writers.* New York: Garland, 1972. Collects reviews of Wordsworth's work; see part A, "The Lake Poets" (2 vols.).

Sheats, Paul D. *The Making of Wordsworth's Poetry, 1785–1798.* Cambridge, Mass.: Harvard University Press, 1973. A study of Wordsworth's early verse.

Stallknecht, Newton P. *Strange Seas of Thought: Studies in William Wordsworth's Philosophy of Man and Nature.* Durham, N.C.: Duke University Press, 1945. Reprinted, Bloomington: Indiana University Press, 1958.

Stein, Edwin. *Wordsworth's Art of Allusion.* University Park: Pennsylvania State University Press, 1988. Examines uses of quotations, echoes, and allusions in Wordsworth's poetry; sees Wordsworth as a literary poet.

Thomson, A. W., ed. *Wordsworth's Mind and Art.* Edinburgh: Oliver & Boyd, 1969. Collects a variety of modern articles, mostly by British critics.

Todd, F. M. *Politics and the Poet: A Study of Wordsworth.* London: Methuen, 1957. Sound study of Wordsworth as a thinking, feeling man of his time.

Whitehead, Alfred North. *Science and the Modern World.* New York: New American Library, 1925. Republished in Mentor Books (paperback), 1948. Notable defense of Wordsworth's philosophy.

Willey, Basil. "On Wordsworth and the Locke Tradition." In *The Seventeenth Century Background.* London: Chatto & Windus, 1934. The English scientific tradition conditioned much of Wordsworth's thought.

_____. *The Eighteenth Century Background.* London: Chatto & Windus, 1940. Continues elucidation of Wordsworth's natural philosophy in its historical context.

Woodring, Carl. *Wordsworth.* Boston: Houghton Mifflin, 1965. A compact scholarly introduction to the poetry and prose.

Wordsworth, Jonathan. *The Music of Humanity: A Critical Study of Wordsworth's "Ruined Cottage."* New York: Harper & Row, 1969. Reconstructs "The Ruined Cottage" from early manuscript into virtually a new poem. Full commentary on its composition, literary background, symbolism, and its relationship to "The Pedlar."

_____. *William Wordsworth: The Borders of Vision.* Oxford: Clarendon, 1982. On Wordsworth's visionary poetry as seen chronologically; uses latest manuscript materials.

Wordsworth, Jonathan. Editor. *Bicentenary Wordsworth Studies in Memory of John Alban Finch.* Ithaca: Cornell University Press, 1970. A wide-ranging series of essays.

Criticism: Lyrical Ballads

Jacobus, Mary. *Tradition and Experiment in Wordsworth's "Lyrical Ballads" (1798)*. Oxford: Oxford University Press, 1976. A discerning study of *Lyrical Ballads* complementing that by Parrish.

Jordan, John. *Why the Lyrical Ballads?* Berkeley: University of California Press, 1976. Deals with the volume in its historical context.

Mayo, Robert. "The Contemporaneity of the *Lyrical Ballads*." *Publications of the Modern Language Association* 69 (1954): 486–522. Places the poems in their historical context, limiting their originality.

Murray, Roger N. *Wordsworth's Style: Figures and Themes in Lyrical Ballads of 1800*. Lincoln: University of Nebraska Press, 1967. Analyses of Wordsworth's language and handling of poetic figures.

Parrish, Stephen Maxfield. *The Art of the "Lyrical Ballads."* Cambridge Mass.: Harvard University Press, 1973. An illuminating account in line with the most recent scholarly discoveries.

Criticism: The Prelude

Bishop, Jonathan. "Wordsworth and the 'Spots of Time.' " *English Literary History* 26 (1959): 45–65. Discusses patterns in nineteen events in *The Prelude* identified as "spots of time."

Havens, Raymond D. *The Mind of a Poet: A Study of Wordsworth's Thought with Particular Reference to "The Prelude."* Baltimore: Johns Hopkins University Press, 1941. Detailed commentary supplements the notes to the de Selincourt edition of *The Prelude*.

LeGuois, Émile. *The Early Life of William Wordsworth, 1770–1798: A Study of "The Prelude,"* translated by J. W. Matthews. London: Dent, 1897. Reprinted with new material, 1921 and 1932. New York: Dutton. The first scholar to place *The Prelude* at the center of Wordsworth's corpus. Much of the historical criticism is still unsuperseded.

Lindenberger, Herbert. *On Wordsworth's Prelude*. Princeton, N.J.: Princeton University Press, 1963. A series of related essays on the poem's language, style, theme, and structure.

Criticism: The Excursion

Lyon, J. S. *The Excursion: A Study*. New Haven: Yale University Press, 1950. Full historical and critical commentary.

Piper, H. W. *The Active Universe: Pantheism and the Concept of the Imagination in the English Romantic Poets*. London: Athlone (University of London), 1962. Has several good chapters on *The Excursion*.

Index

Abrams, M. H., 64, 65
Akenside, Mark, 121
Alfoxden, 23, 35, 36, 37, 41, 46, 47
Arabian Nights, 71, 86
Archimedes, 113
Aristotle, 63, 64
Arnold, Matthew, 64, 120, 139, 141

Bacon, Sir Francis, 131
Bartram's Travels, 54
Bateson, F. W., 49
Beattie, James, 3
Beaumont, Lady, 137, 142
Beaumont, Sir George, 117, 118
Beaupuy, Michel, 7, 8, 10, 13, 72, 83, 87
Beerbohm, Max, 38
British Critic, 46
Browning, Robert, 126
Burger, G. A., 26, 54
Burn, the "Minstrel," 110
Burney, Dr. Charles, 46
Burns, Robert, 101

Calvert, Raisley, 14
Calvert, William, 10, 14
Cambridge, St. John's College, 4, 5, 6, 7, 69, 70, 72, 90, 92
Carroll, Lewis, 103
Chatterton, Thomas, 3, 48, 101, 103
Chaucer, 69, 95, 103, 140
Cockermouth, 1–2
Coleridge, Hartley, 113
Coleridge, Samuel Taylor, 9, 12, 14, 17, 23, 24, 26, 30, 32, 37, 38, 39, 41, 45, 47, 49, 50, 51, 58, 63, 65, 67, 69, 71, 74, 75, 76, 78, 87, 94, 100, 108, 111, 113, 115, 116, 121, 122, 128, 132, 137, 139, 140, 142, "The Ancient Mariner," 24, 26, 28, 32, 33, 34, 45, 46; *Biographia Literaria,* 24, 65, 139;

"Christabel," 24; "The Dungeon," 26; "The Foster Mother's Tale," 26; *The Friend,* 76; "Lewt," 45; "The Nightingale," 26, 45; *Osorio,* 26
Coleridge, Sara, 46
Collins, William, 3, 48
Cookson, William, 5
Cottle, Joseph, 23, 25, 41, 45
Cowper, William, 121
Coxe, William, 8
Crabbe, George, 53, 121, 137
Critical Review, The, 45

Dame, Tyson, 70, 84
Danby, John F., 19
Darwin, Erasmus, 5, 35
Davie, Donald, 92
De Carbonniéres, Ramond, 8
De Selincourt, Ernest, 88
Derwent, River, 1, 68
Don Quixote, 31, 70
Dove Cottage, 58, 59, 67, 104–108
Drayton, Michael, 53, 95
Dryden, John, 140

Fawcett, Joseph, 122
Fenwick, Isabella, 3, 16
Fox, Charles James, 59
French Revolution, 9, 13, 18, 23, 41, 73, 74, 82–83, 84, 94, 96, 124, 142
Furness, Abbey, 69

Gilpin, William, 5, 42, 86
Godwin, William, 12, 13, 14, 16, 38, 39, 74
Goslar, 47, 50, 53, 55
Gray, Thomas, 3
Grob, Alan, 110

Hamilton (Scottish balladist), 110
Harrington, James, 98
Hartman, Geoffrey, 8

157

Wilkinson, Thomas, 108–109
Wilson, John, 32
Wordsworth, Anne (the poet's mother), 1, 2
Wordsworth, Caroline, 96
Wordsworth, Dorothy (the poet's sister), 2, 5, 7, 23, 24, 37, 41, 42, 44, 47, 49, 51, 52, 58, 71, 74, 75, 84, 86, 87, 96, 104, 105, 106, 108, 110, 111, 122
Wordsworth, John (the poet's brother), 100, 117, 118, 119, 130
Wordsworth, John (the poet's son), 133
Wordsworth, John (the poet's father), 1, 74, 81
Wordsworth, Mary Hutchinson, 49, 58, 68, 71, 81, 99, 100, 104, 130, 136
Wordsworth, William

WORKS:
"The Affliction of Margaret," 107
"Afterthought," 120
"Among all lovely things," 49
"Anecdote for Fathers," 37–38
The Borderers, 12, 14–18
"The Brothers," 58–60, 95
"Calais, August 1802," 96
"Calais, August 15, 1802," 97
"The Complaint of a Forsaken Indian Woman," 37
"Composed near Calais," 96, 97
"Composed upon an Evening of Extraordinary Splendour," 135
"The Convict," 26
Descriptive Sketches, 6–9, 11, 139
"Dion," 134–35
Ecclesiastical Sonnets, 136
"Elegiac Stanzas," 96, 116, 117, 119
"Essay, Supplementary to the Preface, 1815," 139
Evening Voluntaries, 135
An Evening Walk, 4, 5, 6, 8
The Excursion, 20, 21, 120–29
"Expostulation and Reply," 39–40
"Fair Star of Evening," 96
"A Farewell," 105
"The Female Vagrant," 10–12, 13, 26, 45

"The Fountain," 56–57
"Goody Blake and Harry Gill," 26, 28, 35–36
"Great Men Have Been Among Us," 98
"The Green Linnet," 106
"Guilt and Sorrow," 9, 10, 20
"The Happy Warrior," 119
"The Idiot Boy," 26, 30–32, 45
"I grieved for Buonaparté," 96
"Influence of Natural Objects," 89
"I Wandered Lonely As a Cloud," 105–106
"King's College Chapel," 136
"Laodamia," 120, 134–35
"The Last of the Flock," 37
"Letter to the Bishop of Llandaff," 9, 11, 13
"Lines Composed a Few Miles above Tintern Abbey," 25, 26, 41–45, 47, 77, 79
"Lines Left upon a Seat in a Yew-tree," 26
"Lines Written in Early Spring," 39, 41
"Lines Written near Richmond," 26
"London, 1802," 97, 99
"Lucy Gray," 47, 52–53
Lucy poems, 47–52
Lyrical Ballads, 10, 23 66, 95, 104, 107, 139
"The Mad Mother," 37, 58
Matthew poems, 47, 55–57
"Michael," 58, 59, 60–63, 95
"Mutability," 120, 136
"My Heart Leaps Up," 111
"Ode: Intimations of Immortality," 38, 96, 110–15, 116, 117, 118, 119, 135
"Ode to Duty," 96, 116–17, 119
"The Old Cumberland Beggar," 18–19
"The Old Man Traveling," 26
"On the Extinction of the Venetian Republic," 97
"On Westminster Bridge," 97
"Peter Bell," 28, 32–35
Poems in Two Volumes, 1807, 95–119
"A Poet's Epitaph," 47, 57–58
Preface *to Lyrical Ballads,* 63–66
The Prelude, 1, 2, 5, 9, 12, 13, 47, 60,

The Authors

Russell Noyes was a distinguished scholar in the field of English romanticism and of Wordsworth in particular. Born in 1901, he received his doctorate from Harvard University in 1932 and taught English at the University of Massachusetts, Boston University, Harvard University, and, for most of his career, Indiana University, where he served as chair of the Department of English from 1941 to 1951. He was chiefly responsible for the continued development of the rich Wordsworth Collection at the Lilly Library of Indiana University, originally gathered by Oscar L. Watkins and described in Professor Noyes's *Indiana Wordsworth Collection: A Catalogue* (1978). Following publication of some specialized scholarly books, *Drayton's Literary Vogue* (1935) and *Wordsworth and Jeffrey in Controversy* (1941), he edited *English Romantic Poetry and Prose* (1956), the most comprehensive and widely used anthology of the period. Throughout his life an active gardener with an undergraduate degree from the University of Massachusetts in landscape architecture, he combined interests and published *Wordsworth and the Art of Landscape* in 1968. His lecture tours took him, among other places, to Japan, where he discovered and encouraged an interest in Wordsworth that is still much in evidence. He died in 1980.

John O. Hayden received his Ph.D. from Columbia University and was a research student at Cambridge University. He entered the field of romantic scholarship by studying the contemporary reception of romantic writers (*The Romantic Reviewers*, 1969). His research interests remained broad; he produced an edition of the nineteenth-century reception of Sir Walter Scott (*Scott: The Critical Heritage*, 1970) and subsequently published scholarly articles on most of the romantic writers, from Coleridge and Byron to Hazlitt and Hunt. More recently, Hayden has focused on William Wordsworth and has edited two volumes of *The Complete Poems*, 1977, and a volume of *The Prose*, 1988, for Penguin Books. His work on the history of literary theory (*Polestar of the Ancients*, 1979), moreover, has allowed him to revise the place of Wordsworth's criticism in that history. Hayden is currently teaching at the University of California, Davis, and has just completed a study of Wordsworth's psychological interests. He is on the board of advisors of the *Wordsworth Circle*.